Gosch
Overbeck-Hellwing
Besch

Mail for You
Englische Handelskorrespondenz

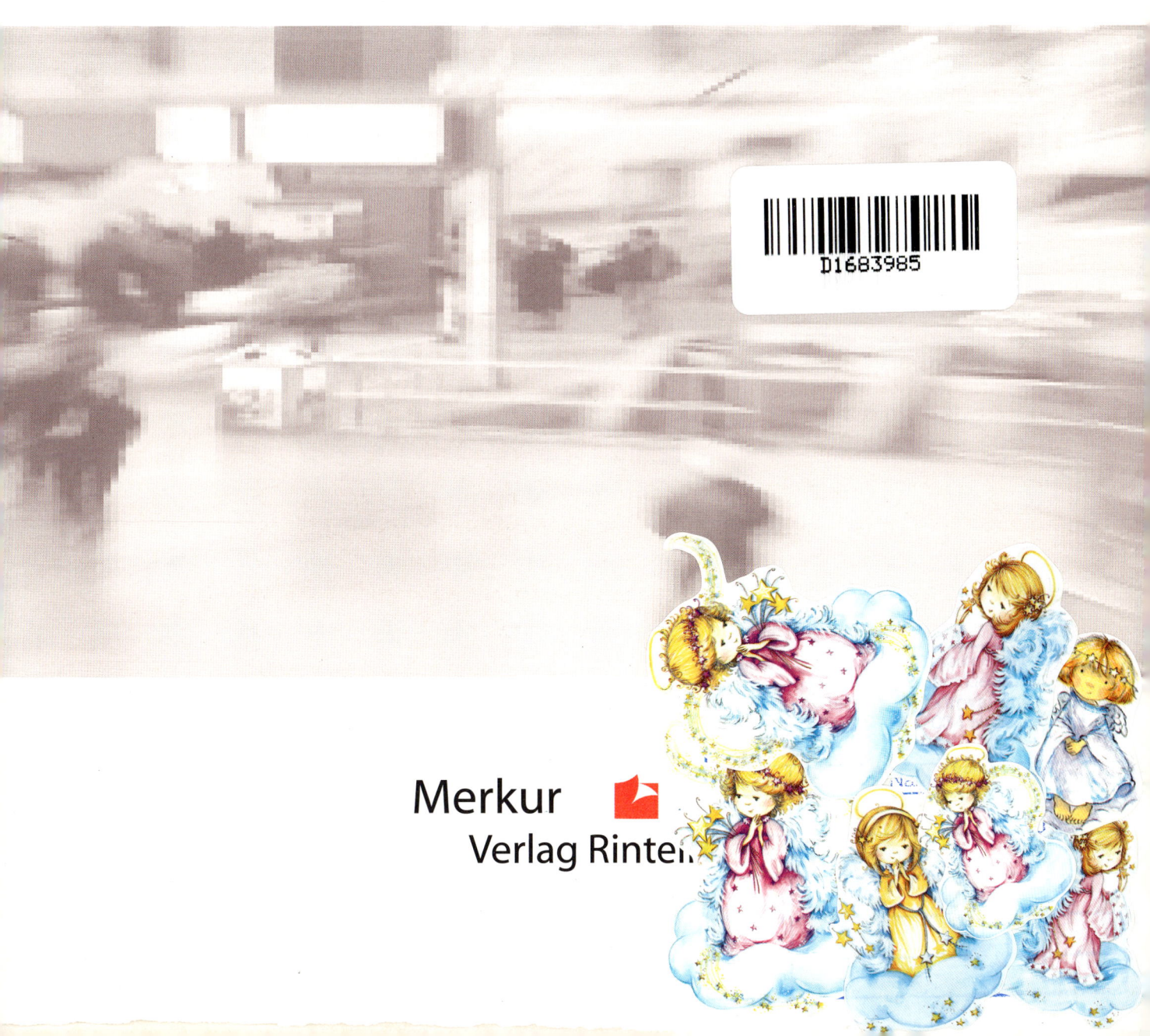

Merkur
Verlag Rinteln

Wirtschaftswissenschaftliche Bücherei für Schule und Praxis
Begründet von Handelsschul-Direktor Dipl.-Hdl. Friedrich Hutkap †

Die Verfasser:

Brigitte Gosch
† 2002

Ruth Overbeck-Hellwing
Lehrerin für die Sekundarstufe II
Direktorin eines Schulzentrums in Bremen

Victor Besch
Diplom-Psychologe B.Sc.,
arbeitet im Diakonischen Krankenhaus, Krankenpflegeschule Rotenburg/Wümme

Das Werk und seine Teile sind urheberrechtlich geschützt. Jede Nutzung in anderen als den gesetzlich zugelassenen Fällen bedarf der vorherigen schriftlichen Einwilligung des Verlages. Hinweis zu § 52 a UrhG: Weder das Werk noch seine Teile dürfen ohne eine solche Einwilligung eingescannt und in ein Netzwerk eingestellt werden. Dies gilt auch für Intranets von Schulen und sonstigen Bildungseinrichtungen.

* * * * *

4. Auflage 2012
© 2000 by MERKUR VERLAG RINTELN

Gesamtherstellung:
MERKUR VERLAG RINTELN Hutkap GmbH & Co. KG, 31735 Rinteln
E-Mail: info@merkur-verlag.de
         lehrer-service@merkur-verlag.de
Internet: www.merkur-verlag.de

ISBN 978-3-8120-0847-1

Vorwort

MAIL FOR YOU
ist ein Kursbuch, das in die englische Handelskorrespondenz einführt. Es wendet sich insbesondere an Lernende und Anwender ohne oder mit geringen Vorkenntnissen in diesem Bereich.

Ziel dieses Kurses ist, den Lernenden in die Lage zu versetzen, einfache Briefe im Geschäftsverkehr aus den Bereichen

- *enquiry* (Anfrage)
- *offer* (Angebot)
- *order* (Bestellung)
- *order acknowledgement* (Auftragsbestätigung)
- *complaints* (Beschwerden)

in verständlichem und korrektem *Business English* zu entwerfen.

Die fünf aufeinander aufbauenden Kapitel des Kurses stellen eine Kombination aus Lernen und Anwenden dar.

Jedes Kapitel beginnt mit einem einführenden Lesebeispiel, das anschließend inhaltlich bearbeitet wird. In den folgenden Übungsbriefen wird auf das bereits erworbene Wissen zurückgegriffen. Neue Inhalte werden in kleinen Schritten entfaltet. Dabei werden besondere im Geschäftsverkehr gebräuchliche Vokabeln sowie verständliche und für eigene Korrespondenzen leicht modifizierbare Redewendungen eingeführt. Die Anwendung der verschiedenen Korrespondenzen wird in mehreren Sequenzen geübt und gefestigt. Ergänzende Übungen in Form von Wortgitterrätseln trainieren spielerisch das Vokabelgedächtnis.

Die für das Schreiben von Handelskorrespondenz wichtigen Grammatikregeln werden detailliert erläutert und ihre Anwendung in besonderen Übungen gefestigt.

Die Kapitel sind in den Themen und Beispielen aufeinander bezogen. Sinnvollerweise sollte der Kurs in der dargebotenen Reihenfolge fortlaufend bearbeitet werden.

Die Kursmaterialien sind mehrfach in berufsbildenden Lehrgängen für kaufmännische Berufe erprobt und verbessert worden. Anregungen und Verbesserungsvorschläge sind uns für die Weiterentwicklung des Kurskonzeptes sehr willkommen. Für die dritte Auflage bedanken wir uns herzlich bei Herrn Peter Schwirtz für seine hilfreichen Anmerkungen.

E-Mail: overbeck-hellwing@t-online.de, pipemager@crest-of-gordon.de

Wir wünschen den Nutzern des Kurses viel Freude beim Lernen und Anwenden.

Die Verfasser

Contents

				page
Unit 1:	**Layout of a letter**			7
Unit 2:	**Enquiries - Inquiries**			11
	Introduction			11
	Letter 1	The Bike Shop	→ Das Rad	13
	Letter 2	Das Rad	→ Lung Mingh	16
	Letter 3	Sportmexx	→ Sport und Spaß	19
	Language Practice	Present Tenses		21
	Letter 4	Vobas	→ Compatec	28
	Letter 5	Das Rad	→ Telcom	34
	A Telephone Call			37
	Language Practice	Will-Future		41
	Crossword			46
	Useful Phrases			48
Unit 3:	**Offers**			50
	Introduction			50
	Letter 1	Das Rad	→ The Bike Shop	52
	Letter 2	Lungh Mingh	→ Das Rad	56
	Language Practice	The Passive		60
	Letter 3	Sport und Spaß	→ Sportmexx	64
	Letter 4	Compatec	→ Vobas	68
	Letter 5	Telcom	→ Das Rad	74
	A Telephone Call			76
	Language Practice	Present Perfect		78
	Crossword			80
	Useful Phrases			82
Unit 4:	**Orders**			85
	Introduction			85
	Letter 1	The Bike Shop	→ Das Rad	87
	Language Practice	Simple Past		90
	Letter 2	Das Rad	→ Lung Mingh	92
	Letter 3	Sportmexx	→ Sport und Spaß	96
	Letter 4	Vobas	→ Compatec	100
	Letter 5	Das Rad	→ Telcom	102
	A Telephone Call			106
	Crossword			109
	Useful Phrases			110

Unit 5: Acknowledgements and dispatch notes

Introduction			112
Letter 1	Das Rad	→ The Bike Shop	113
Letter 2	Lungh Mingh	→ Das Rad	115
Letter 3	Sport und Spaß	→ Sportmexx	118
Letter 4	Compatec	→ Vobas	120
Letter 5	Telcom	→ Das Rad	124
A Telephone Call			129
Crossword			131
Useful Phrases			132

Unit 6: Complaints

Introduction			134
Letter 1	The Bike Shop	→ Das Rad	135
Letter 2	Das Rad	→ Lung Mingh	138
Letter 3	Sportmexx	→ Sport und Spaß	140
Letter 4	Vobas	→ Compatec	144
Letter 5	Das Rad	→ Telcom	146
A Telephone Call			149
Crossword			152
Useful Phrases			153
Vocabulary			154

The symbols used in this book ask you to

 read   and    write.

UNIT ONE: LAYOUT OF A LETTER

```
4   The Bike Shop                          Das Rad GmbH
    27 Brompton Road                       Breite Straße 12
    LONDON SW 11                           28325 Bremen       1
    ENGLAND                         Tel: +49  421  361-18263
                                    Fax: +49  421  361-18264

                                    Your ref:   CL/dm
                                    Our ref:    PvZ/dl         2
                                    Date:       24 August 2010 3

5   (For the attention of the Sales Manager)*

6   Dear Mr Clease

7   Offer for bicycles

    Thank you for your enquiry of 16 August 2010.

    Please find enclosed our latest catalogue, price and terms of business.

    The prices quotet are FOB Bremen and shipment can be arranged immediatley after receipt of order.

8   We are willing to grant retail discounts of 15% on the net price.

    As we have not done business before we request payments by irrevocable and confirmed letter of credit.

    We hope that our prices and terms meet with your approval and that you will decide to place your order with us.

9   Yours sincerely
    Das Rad GmbH

10  Patrick von Zahn
    Patrick von Zahn
    Sales Manager

11  Enclosures
```

When you look at the letter above you will see that it consists of **various** different **parts**:

1. **Letterhead:** It shows the name of the company, its address, telephone- and fax number etc. The letterhead may vary from company to company; the above letterhead is only an example. Letterheads from German companies usually look different. (see page 29)
2. **References:** They tell you who is responsible for the letter (Patrick von Zahn) and who actually wrote the letter (e.g. the secretary Deborah Lewis).
3. **Date:** This shows the day the letter was written.
4. **Inside address:** It shows the name of the company/person you are writing to.
5. **Attention line:** It is used in a letter to a company and is meant to be read by a particular person. * only used if name is not known (mainly in enquiries)
6. **Opening salutation:** Greeting to the addressee (person/company you are writing to).
7. **Subject line:** It tells the addressee what the letter is about. This should be <u>underlined</u> or written in **bold** script.
8. **Body of the letter:** This is the actual message.
9. **Complimentary close:** Final greeting to the addressee.
10. **Signature block:** Shows the name of the writer/sender of the letter and his position in the firm e.g. Purchasing Manager etc.
11. **Enclosure(s)/enc(s):** They tell the addressee that additional material (catalogue etc.) has been sent.

7

Let us have a look at two important things in business letters.

1. The Date

Look at the example letter and how the date is written there: 24 August 2010 (day, month, year) You may of course write 24th August 2010 but you should only use *st, nd, rd, th* if you are absolutely sure when to use them.

Note: In America the date is written in a different way. They write the month first and then the day and year. So 2/8/00 is the 2$^{(nd)}$ August 2010 in England but the February 8, 2010 in America.

 **How would you write the dates below in a letter?**

28.10.15 _____

3/8/99 (England) _____

2$^{(nd)}$ April 13 _____

Feb. 1$^{(st)}$, 2010 _____

2. Opening Salutation/Complimentary Close

The way you close a letter depends on how you open it.

Here are some ways to open a business letter:

Dear Madam	to a woman
Dear Sir	to a man
Dear Sir or Madam	to a company
Dear Mr Gibson	to a man
Dear Mrs Langer	to a married woman
Dear Ms Müller	to a woman if you do not know if she is married **Note:** This should be used, because more and more women prefer this.
Dear Miss Simon	to an unmarried woman **Note:** This can be seen as impolite and so should not be used.
Dear Paul	to a close business partner

This is how you close a letter:

Dear Madam
Dear Sir } Yours faithfully
Dear Sir or Madam

8

Dear Mr Gibson
Dear Mrs Langer   } Yours sincerely
Dear Ms Müller
Dear Miss Simon

Dear Paul   } Best wishes

Which closings go with these openings?

	Yours faithfully	Yours sincerely	Best wishes
Dear Madam	☐	☐	☐
Dear Mrs Dearns	☐	☐	☐
Dear Ms Rosenbrock	☐	☐	☐
Dear Sharon	☐	☐	☐
Dear Sir or Madam	☐	☐	☐
Dear Mr Clease	☐	☐	☐
Dear Gaby	☐	☐	☐

3. Writing numbers in German and English

When we write 'thousand' in English, we use a comma – i.e. 1,000 and in German we use a full stop – i.e. 1.000! In terms of money, we might have to pay 'one thousand pounds and fifty pence'. In English we would then write: 1,000.50 £ – in German: 1.000,50 £.

Note: The commas and full stops are the other way round!

A modern way of laying out a business letter is used in this book. It is called 'block style'.

If you look at the letter on page 7 again you will see that
- the inside address is at the top on the left
- the references can be at the top on the right
- the date is under the references
- there are no commas after 'Dear Sir' and 'Yours faithfully'
- there are line spaces between the paragraphs of the letter
- all paragraphs start at the left margin
- the writer's name is printed under his/her signature
- (sometimes) the writer's title (position in the company) e.g. 'Sales Manager' is written under his/her printed name

 **Fill in the crossword by finding suitable words for the gaps below.**

1.
2.
3.
4.
5.
6.
7.
8.
9.
10.

1. You write _____ at the end of the letter to let the reader know that additional material (brochure, price list etc) has been sent.

2. The _____ is the person or company who writes the letter.

3. If you want e.g. the Sales Manager in a company to get the letter quickly but you do not know his or her name you write an _____ .

4. The _____ shows the name of the writer of the letter and (sometimes) his position in the firm; e.g. Sales Manager.

5. At the beginning of the letter you write the _____ to greet the

6. _____ .

7. The actual message of the letter is the _____ .

8. When you want to finish a letter you write the _____ as a final greeting to the addressee.

9. The way the letter is structured, how it is made up, is called the _____

10. The _____ shows when the letter was written.

11. There is a hidden word in the box. What does it mean? Give a short description.

_____

_____

_____

10

UNIT TWO: ENQUIRIES - INQUIRIES

If you look up the word *'enquire'* in a good dictionary, you will find something like: *to ask about something;* or *to seek information by questioning.* You will find something very similar under *'inquire'* – so you could say both words **enquire and inquire are the same.** The noun-form is 'the enquiry' or 'the inquiry'.

You must now decide which version you want to use *Enquire* or *Inquire;* and **stick to it. Do not** change the spelling of words!

If you want to buy goods or services you need information first. Your starting point should therefore be **a letter of enquiry.**

There are two types of letters of enquiry:

(a) **General Enquiry:** These letters ask for some information about the company you are writing to: *What products can they offer you? What are the prices, terms of payment and delivery?* You could also ask the company to send you a catalogue, samples and further information. It is often a good idea to ask about discounts, especially if you are thinking about placing a big order.

(b) **Special Enquiry:** If you write a special enquiry, you want to know about a particular service or product. You might have to describe the product you want and ask if the company can supply it – especially if you have special wishes e.g. technical data or size. You should tell them exactly what you want and in what quantity and then ask about the price. It is a good idea to check if the seller offers special terms and conditions, especially if you are interested in placing further orders or entering into deeper business relations. When the company has received your letter of enquiry they know what you want and can make you an offer.

Now we know what to include in our letter of enquiry. What about the structure of the letter? Be polite in your letter, so start by saying where you got their address from e.g.: *We saw your advertisement in ...; You were recommended to us by ... etc.* You should then explain who you are and what you are interested in. Ask about terms e.g. *Could you please let us have your terms of business etc.*

With this information the addressee will be able to build up a picture and then find ways of helping you. Again, your letter should close with a polite sentence such as: *We look forward to hearing from you ...;* or: *We hope to hear from you in due course.*

 **Mark the following points as *general enquiry* (ge) or *special enquiry* (se) or *both* (b).**

		ge	se	b
1.	If you enquire about discounts, it is (a)	☐	☐	☐
2.	If it says where you got the address from, it is (a)	☐	☐	☐
3.	If a catalogue is requested, it is (a)	☐	☐	☐
4.	If you tell the addressee who you are, it is (a)	☐	☐	☐
5.	If you have special wishes, it is (a)	☐	☐	☐
6.	If you request samples, it is (a)	☐	☐	☐
7.	If someone wants to know the price, it is (a)	☐	☐	☐
8.	If there is a salutation, it is (a)	☐	☐	☐
9.	If someone wants to know the terms of payment, it is (a)	☐	☐	☐
10.	If you want to know if a particular product is available, it is (a)	☐	☐	☐
11.	If you want to know the technical data, it is (a)	☐	☐	☐
12.	If you want a description of the product you want, it is (a)	☐	☐	☐
13.	If you want to know what products are available, it is (a)	☐	☐	☐
14.	If you want to know the terms of delivery, it is (a)	☐	☐	☐

Now summarize what belongs to a general enquiry or a special enquiry.

general enquiry	special enquiry

The Bike Shop

Das Rad GmbH
Breite Straße 12
28325 BREMEN
GERMANY

27 Brompton Road
London SW 11
Phone 01 370-2197
Fax   01 370-2198

Your ref:
Our ref: JC/dl
Date:

Dear Sir or Madam

Enquiry

We refer to our visit to your company's stand at the recent bicycle fair IFMA in Cologne.

We are a well-established retailer of bicycles specializing in high-quality mountain bikes.

As the market for mountain-bikes is steadily increasing in Britain, we are interested in developing wider sources of supply.

We would therefore be grateful, if you could send us your current catalogue and price list. Please let us also have details of your terms and retail discounts.

We look forward to hearing from you soon.

Yours faithfully

John Clease
John Clease
Purchasing Manager

Questions
a) Who is the letter from?
b) Who is the letter to?
c) Where did the sender get the address from?
d) What does the sender want *Das Rad GmbH* to do?
e) What is the sender interested in?

The Bike Shop

Das Rad GmbH
Breite Straße 12
28325 BREMEN
GERMANY

257 Brompton Road
London SW 11
Phone 01 370-2197
Fax   01 370-2198

Your ref:
Our ref: JC/dl

 **Fill in the gaps.**

Dear Sir or Madam

Enquiry

We_____ to our _____ to your company's _____ at the recent _____ IFMA in Cologne.

We are a well-established _____ of bicycles _____ in _____-quality mountain bikes.

As the _____ for mountain bikes is steadily _____ in Britain, we are _____ in _____ wider sources of _____.

We would _____ be grateful, if you _____ send us your current _____ and price list. Please_____ us also _____ details of your terms and retail _____.

We_____ forward to _____ from you soon.

_____ faithfully

John Clease

John Clease

Purchasing Manager

Choose the right words from the box and fill in the gaps:

retailer	Einzelhändler	to develop	entwickeln, hier: erschließen
to specialize in	sich auf etw. spezialisieren	catalogue	Katalog
high	hoch, hier: hochwertig	to let s.o. have s.th.	jdm. etwas zur Verfügung stellen
to refer to	sich beziehen auf	discount	Rabatt
visit	Besuch	market	Markt
stand	Stand (auf Messe)	to increase	größer werden, sich erhöhen
bicycle fair	Fahrradmesse	to be interested in	interessiert sein an
could (Past can)	konnte, hier: könnten	supply	Versorgung, Lieferung
therefore	deshalb, deswegen	to look forward to	sich freuen auf
yours	dein, Ihr (Grußformel im Brief)	to hear	hören

 **Which prepositions go with these words?**

a) We refer _____ your letter _____ 20 October _____.

b) We visited your stand _____ the recent bicycle fair _____ London.

c) We are a retailer _____ casual wear.

d) We specialize _____ high-quality clothes.

e) We are specialized _____ shoes and trousers.

f) Could you please give us details _____ your terms and retail discounts.

g) We are interested _____ gett_____ more information _____ your products.

h) We look forward _____ hear_____ from you soon.

Crossword

3↓ 1→   2↓

1 erhöhen
2 anfragen, erkundigen
  essen
  das (da)
  Geschäftsbedingungen
  spezialisiert

3 interessiert
  entwickeln
  Preise
  Marktstand
  Detail, Einzelheit
  Land

15

Das Rad GmbH
Breite Straße 12
28325 Bremen
Tel: +49 421 361-18263
Fax: +49 421 361-18264

Lung Mingh Ltd
23 Xingh-Mu
BEIJING
REPUBLIC OF CHINA

Ihr Zeichen:　　　　　Unser Zeichen: IL/dl　　　　　Bremen,

Dear Sir or Madam

Enquiry for dynamos

We refer to your _____ in this week's edition __ Biker's Magazine.

__ are _ medium - _____ manufacturer __ bicycles __ Germany ___ we ____ to _____ wider _____ of _____ .
We are particularly _____ in the dynamo FX 37 that you offer.

We _____ therefore __ pleased, __ you _____ let __ have ____ prices and a brochure on your _____ . Could ___ also ____ us ___ of ____ FX 37 dynamos ___ testing.

_____ let __ know ____ terms __ business _____ with _____ about _____ .

We ____ to ____ from ___ in ___ near _____ .

Yours _____

Inge Langer
Inge Langer
Purchasing Manager

Choose the right words from the box and fill in the gaps:

a - advertisement - and - be - could - details - develop - discounts - dynamos - faithfully - for - future - hear - hope - if - in - interested - of - of - of - one - please - send - sized - sources - supply - the - together - us - us - want - we - would - you - you - your - your - your

Crossword

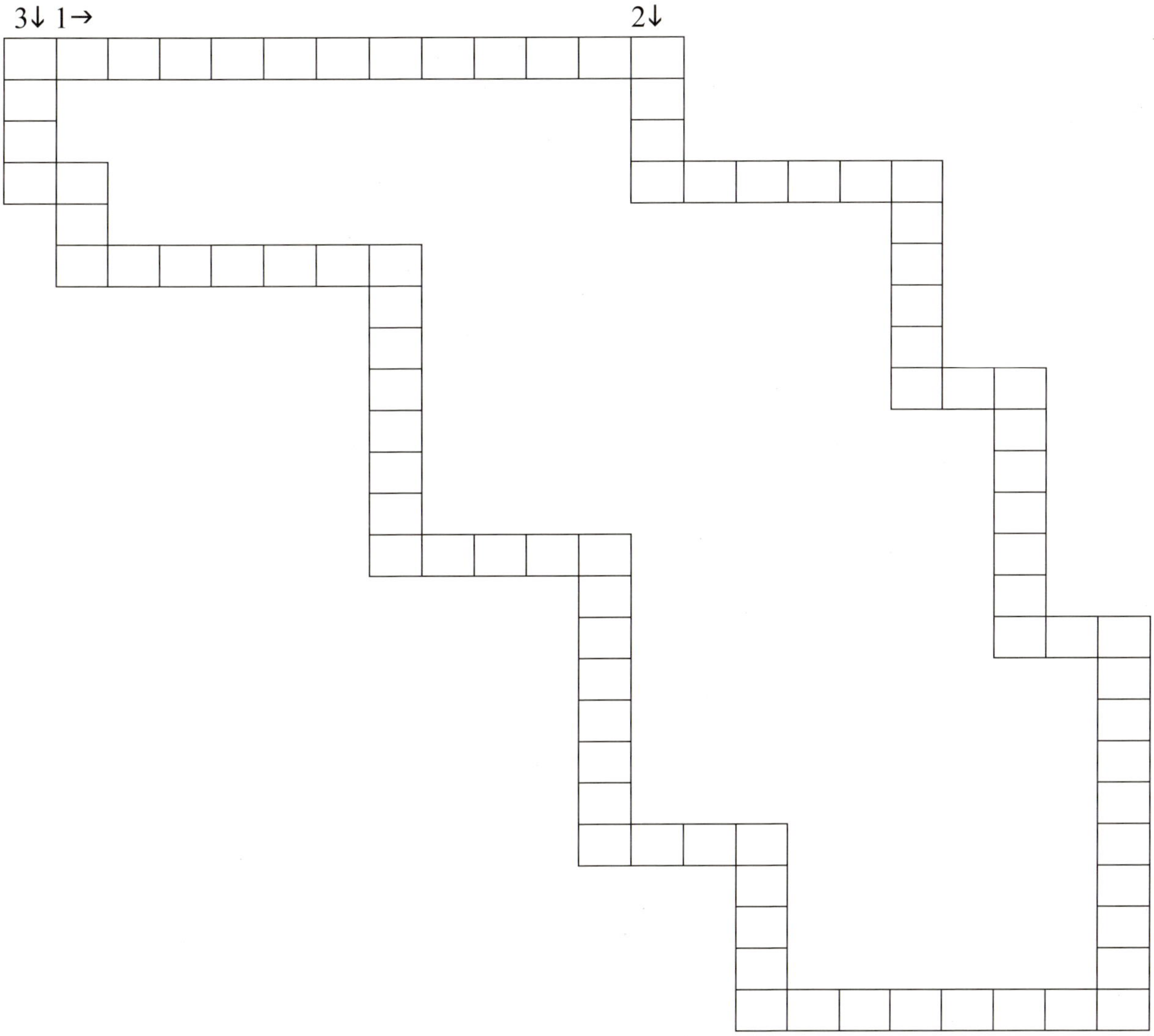

3↓ 1→ 2↓

1
Werbung, Anzeige
2
Mannschaft, Team
mittel
Markt
der, die, das
Ausgabe (von Zeitung)
jetzt
Großhändler

3
so, auch
von, aus
für
Grüße
Lieferant
Straße (Mz.)
ständig
dein, deine
(sich) beziehen (auf)
Einzelhändler

 **Was sagen/schreiben Sie, wenn**

a) Sie sich auf etwas beziehen?

b) Sie sich als mittelständisches Unternehmen vorstellen wollen?

c) Sie sich größere Bezugsquellen erschließen wollen?

d) Sie dankbar wären, wenn Ihnen der aktuelle Katalog geschickt würde?

e) Sie um die Zusendung der Geschäftsbedingungen bitten?

f) Sie sich darauf freuen, von Ihrem Geschäftspartner zu hören?

g) Sie hoffen, bald von Ihrem Geschäftspartner zu hören?

h) Sie sich besonders für die angebotenen Dynamos interessieren?

i) Sie sich auf die Anzeige in der Ausgabe des *Business Today* von dieser Woche beziehen?

j) Sie darum bitten, die aktuelle Preisliste geschickt zu bekommen?

k) Ihnen die Firma XY von der Firma Z empfohlen wurde?

 **Draft a letter and structure it correctly.**

Sie heißen Sharon Dearns und arbeiten bei der Firma *Sportmexx*. Schreiben Sie eine Anfrage an die Firma *Sport + Spaß*, Walliser Straße 125, 28325 Bremen.
- Teilen Sie mit, dass Sie sich freuen würden, bald von *Sport + Spaß* zu hören.
- Sie sind ein führender Großhändler für Sportbekleidung und möchten sich weitere Bezugsquellen erschließen.
- Grußformel
- Bitten Sie um Zusendung des aktuellen Katalogs, der Preisliste und einiger Muster der von *Sport + Spaß* hergestellten Sportbekleidung.
- Beziehen Sie sich auf Ihren Besuch des Messestandes der Firma *Sport + Spaß* auf der letzten Messe *Sport and Leisure* in Birmingham.

Sportmexx
43 Station Road
Fakenham
Norfolk NR 12 7 GH
Tel: 876620   Fax: 886620

Your ref:
Our ref:
Date:

 **Fill in the table with suitable verbs and nouns.**

Nouns	Verbs	Nouns	Verbs
manufacturer			to refer
supplier			to advertise
enquiry			to know
hope			to develop
test			to offer
recommendation			to visit

 **Now make up sentences and use the words from above.**

Example:

1. *DaimlerChrysler* **manufacture** *high-quality cars.*

2. _____

3. _____

4. _____

5. _____

6. _____

7. *With **reference** to yesterday's telephone conversation, we would like to place the following order:*

8. _____

9. _____

10. _____

11. _____

12. _____

Language Practice

Letters of enquiry are usually written in the present tense. The present tense is divided into two types: **simple present** and **present continuous.** What is the difference between the two?

SIMPLE PRESENT TENSE

You should try to remember **4 key-words:**

- general   (allgemein)
- permanent   (ständig)
- repeated   (wiederholt)
- the perception (Wahrnehmung)

We use **the simple present tense** when things are **general**:
   We refer to our visit to your company's stand at the fair in Cologne.

We use the **simple present tense** when things are **permanent**:
   The bike sales department is on the second floor.

We use the **simple present tense** for actions which are **repeated**:
   Our Head Office always deals with all enquiries.

We use the **simple present tense** when the actions are: to see, to smell, to hear, to taste – but be careful; these actions must refer to perception (Wahrnehmung)!
   The boss can hear his secretaries' voices over the intercom (Gegensprechanlage).

To use this tense correctly you must also remember:

> He, she, it – the '**s**' must fit!

This means every time the third person singular is the subject of your sentence, you must add the letter '**s**'
   The Sales Manager [he] *signs all business correspondence.*
   The secretary [she] *types all business correspondence.*
   The bicycle [it] *needs new tyres.*

Do you know what 'The Subject' of a sentence is?

The **subject** is simply the person or thing that does the action. In our 3 sentences above, the subjects are:

(1) _____

(2) _____

(3) _____   and all the actions (verbs) end in '**s**'.

 **Now write down 3 examples of the simple present tense from the letters in this unit.**

(1) _____ .

(2) _____ .

(3) _____ .

PRESENT CONTINUOUS TENSE

To use this tense correctly you should try to remember **2 key-words:**

- now   (jetzt)
- future meaning   (zukünftige Bedeutung)

We use the **present continuous tense** when an action **is happening now:**
*The market for mountain-bikes **is** increas**ing**.*

We use the **present continuous tense** when an action **will happen shortly:**
*The manager **is** fly**ing** to London this evening.*

You can see the difference to the **simple present tense** in the form of your sentences. Remember, in the simple present tense we add the letter '**s**' to the action; in present continuous we have to:

> Use the verb '**to be**' – and add '**-ing**' to the action.

Now look at the two examples above and make sure you understand:

- Who the subject is and
- what form of the verb 'to be' you must use for that subject.

NOTE: The verb '**to be**' is irregular, so learn and remember the following:

Grammatical Person	Form
I	am
you	are
he – she – it	is
we	are
you	are
they	are

There is one **big** danger that people face when learning to use the present continuous tense. People think when they see ...**ing**, it **must** be continuous.

This is a big mistake.

Have another look at the letter on page 13. You will see the following sentences:

*We are a well-established retailer of bicycles **specializing** in high-quality mountain bikes.*
*We are interested in **developing** wider sources of supply.*
*We look forward to **hearing** from you soon.*

Yes, the words specializ**ing,** develop**ing** and hear**ing** all end with the letters '**ing**' – but the sentences are **not** present continuous!

These words are called **Gerunds**. Gerunds are verbs that become nouns by adding '**ing**'.

Just think of the sign you have all seen:

   NO SMOK**ING**

This is *not present continuous* because there is *no* form of the verb '*to be*' in the statement!

Wouldn't the sign sound stupid, if it said   No is smoking?   or   No are smoking?   ?

In this case you can 'feel' that something is wrong; – and you **know** why!
This book aims to get you to know the correct way to draft your business correspondence and avoid making mistakes.

 **Language Practice**

Put the verbs and phrases in brackets into the correct form.

(1) I can't answer the phone, I (*make some photocopies*).
___

(2) The motorway (*run*) from London to Lincoln.
___

(3) My boss (*read*) twenty letters of enquiry every month.
___

(4) I must go now. The manager (*wait*) for me in the conference room.
___

(5) The planet Earth (*move*) round the Sun.
___

(6) The water (*boil*); would you like another cup of tea?
___

(7) Water (*boil*) at 100°C.
___

(8) What (*all managers, do*) at meetings? – They (*discuss*) business proposals.
___

(9) How often (*you, go*) to trade fairs? – I (*visit*) one a month.
___

(10) Where's my secretary? – She (*make*) coffee in the kitchen.
___

A bit of humour:

The boss is sitting in his office and his intercom is switched on. Suddenly he hears a funny noise from the typing pool. He knows there are two secretaries in the room, so he asks:

Boss: 'Miss Jones, what are you doing?'
Miss Jones: 'Nothing, Mr. Davis'.
He doesn't really believe this answer, so he asks:
Boss: '...and Miss Evans; what are you doing?'
Miss Evans: 'Oh! I'm helping Miss Jones.'

 **Points for study and discussion:**

Look at the text and dialogue above.

Why have we used the present continuous tense in the first sentence and simple present in the second?

_____

_____

Why does the boss ask his questions in the present continuous tense?

_____

What tense is the sentence: 'He doesn't really believe this answer'?

_____

Is the sentence positive or negative?

_____

Why is Miss Evans' answer funny?

_____

Why would you lose the joke, if she answered in the simple present tense?

_____

Sometimes when you make an enquiry, or make a telephone call, you must:

- ask a **question**
- say **no** - or
- make an action **negative**

Note: If you need to **say no,** or **ask a question,** you should **use** the verb **'to do'**. For example:

(1) **Do** you smoke? – No, I **don't**.
(2) **Does** your brother live in London? – No, he **doesn't**.
(3) **Do** your sisters snore? – No, they **don't**.

Translate the following questions into English and answer them.

(1) Fahren Sie mit dem Bus zur Arbeit? _____

_____

(2) Verschickt Ihr Kollege viele Faxe? _____

_____

(3) Bekommt Ihre Kollegin viele Anfragen? _____

_____

Notice the other ways that you can say **'no'** or **ask questions**.

(1) **Are** you over 18? – No, I **am not** (I'm not).
(2) **Have** you got a brother? – No, I **have not** (I **haven't**).
(3) **Will** you go now? – No, I **will not** (I **won't**).

Note: If your negative sentence or question uses the verb **'to be'** you **do not use** the verb **'to do'**
The same is true for **'have got'** and **'will'** e.g.

*Enquiries **are not** legally binding.*

 **Translate the following questions into English and answer them.**

(1) Hat sie Hunger? _____

_____

(2) Haben Sie einen netten Chef? _____

_____

(3) Wird Ihre Kollegin viele Anfragen schreiben? _____

_____

Make the following sentences negative.

(1) The secretary writes enquiries.   The boss _____

(2) Managers read a lot.   My grandparents _____

(3) My neighbour plays the piano.   I _____

(4) Some people read the *Financial Times*.   Children _____

(5) Birds fly.   Pigs _____

(6) We are a well-established firm.   *Popeye PLC* _____

(7) Our firm has got many branches.   *Popeye PLC* _____

(8) We will answer your enquiry soon.   A bad company _____

(9) Our fax machine is reliable.   The cheap model _____

(10) Play that tune again!   _____

(11) We can deliver in three weeks.   We _____

(12) The firm accepts cheques.   *Popeye PLC* _____

(13) The secretary is making a telephone call.   Her colleague _____

(14) We have got time to check your references. We _____

 **Draft a letter by putting the phrases from the chart below into the correct order.**

Sie sind Eva Müller, Mitarbeiterin der Firma *Vobas Computers* und schreiben eine Anfrage an die Firma *Compatec*, 35 Mosley Street, London SW 1.
- Teilen Sie mit, dass Sie die Homepage von *Compatec* im Internet gesehen haben und dass Sie besonders an den angebotenen Soundkarten und Lautsprechern interessiert sind.
- Stellen Sie Ihre Firma vor als bekannte Einzelhandelskette für Computer mit Filialen überall in Deutschland.
- Da die Nachfrage nach hochwertigen Heimcomputern schnell wächst, suchen Sie neue Lieferanten für Computerbauteile.
- Sie wären daher dankbar, wenn *Compatec* Ihnen die niedrigsten Preise anbieten könnte für: 1.000 Sound Cards XXF und 1.500 Multimedia Speaker Systems.
- Sie möchten darauf hinweisen, dass die Lieferung per Luftfracht zu erfolgen hat.
- Bitten Sie ebenfalls um Informationen über Geschäftsbedingungen.
- Wenn Preise und Rabatte Ihren Erwartungen entsprechen, werden Sie regelmäßig umfangreiche Aufträge erteilen. Teilen Sie mit, dass Sie sich freuen, bald ein Angebot von *Compatec* zu erhalten.
- Grußformel

	Dear Sir or Madam		new suppliers for components.
	Our company is		retail chain for computers
	your home page on the Internet and		are particularly interested
	We would therefore		be grateful if you could
	that delivery should be made		by air freight.
	a well-known		high-quality home computers
	As the demand for		with branches all over Germany.
	terms of business.		If your prices and discounts
	Please let us also have		information about your
	1,500 Multimedia Speaker Systems		quote us the lowest prices for
	in the sound cards and loudspeaker systems		that you offer.
	is increasing at a fast rate		we are looking for
	Enquiry for computer components		We have seen
	regular substantial orders with you.		We look forward to
	1,000 Sound Cards XXF (and)		We would like to point out
	meet our expectations		we will place
	receiving your offer shortly.		Yours faithfully

28

VOBAS COMPUTERS

Pappelstraße 54
28199 Bremen
Tel: +49 421 2592923

Ihre Zeichen					Unsere Zeichen					Bremen,

 **Choose the right definition and match it with the correct translation.**

1 retail chain	a	a chain you put around a horse's tail	1	hinweisen/auf-
	b	retailer with many shops		merksam machen auf
	c	a chain bracelet a retailer wears		
2 branch	a	late breakfast	2	Geschäfts-
	b	a not well-led farm in the USA		bedingungen
	c	local office or shop that belongs to a large firm		
3 increase	a	to become greater in quantity or size	3	bald
	b	financial or political crisis in a particular country		
	c	big ink spot		
4 point out	a	to direct attention to s.th.	4	Komponente,
	b	a meeting point out in the country		Bestandteil
	c	point in a cricket stadium where the ball is *out*		
5 air freight	a	another word for *fear of flying*	5	Zweigstelle
	b	delivery of goods by plane		
	c	short for *being frightened by air*		
6 terms of business	a	any of the 4 terms of a year when companies do business	6	Luftfracht
	b	conditions relating to selling s.th.		
	c	high buildings where many firms have their businesses		
7 shortly	a	very short pants	7	Bedürfnis, Bedarf,
	b	nickname for a very tiny person		Anspruch
	c	another word for *soon*		
8 component	a	family name of *Al Capone* before he shortened it	8	Lautsprecher
	b	s.b. who composes songs		
	c	any of the parts of which sth is made		
9 requirement	a	group of male singers who only sing at the rear of concert halls	9	zunehmen, erhöht werden
	b	a thing that is depended on or needed		
	c	s.th. you want back		
10 substantial	a	large in amount or value	10	beträchtlich,
	b	a small building where you can seek shelter		erheblich
	c	newspaper stand in a subway station in the USA		
11 loudspeaker	a	s.b. who speaks very loudly	11	Einzelhandelskette
	b	spokesman of the British Parliament		
	c	part of a Hi-Fi system etc. that changes electrical signals into sound		

 **Now write down the words from the previous exercise with their definitions and translations.**

	Word	Definition	Translation
1			
2			
3			
4			
5			
6			
7			
8			
9			
10			
11			

 **Was sagen/schreiben Sie, wenn**

a) Sie die Homepage der anzuschreibenden Firma im Internet gelesen haben?

b) Sie sich als bekannter Lieferant vorstellen möchten?

c) Sie dankbar wären, wenn man Ihnen die niedrigsten Preise nennt?

d) Sie darauf hinweisen möchten, dass …?

e) Sie Informationen über die Allgemeinen Geschäftsbedingungen der Firma erbitten?

f) Sie regelmäßig Bestellungen aufgeben werden?

g) Sie sich besonders für die angebotenen Soundkarten interessieren?

h) Sie erwarten, dass sich der Markt für hochwertige PCs schnell ausweitet?

Crossword

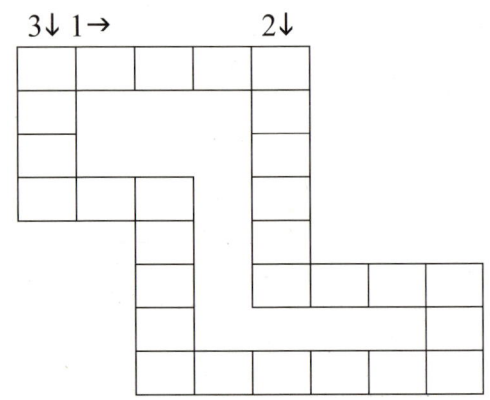

1 (Verkaufs-)Stand
2 Detail
  Liste
  versuchen, probieren

3 schicken, senden
  Tag
  Ihr/Ihre (im Brief)
  Belieferung

Test your vocabulary!
Match the German sentences with the English expressions

Wir wären dankbar, wenn	We are a well-known retail chain.
Wir möchten darauf hinweisen, dass	We have got plants in different North European countries.
Wir sind besonders an ... interessiert.	We will place an order.
Wir sind eine bekannte Einzelhandelskette.	We would be grateful, if
Wir werden eine Bestellung aufgeben.	We are particularly interested in …
Die Lieferung soll per Luftfracht erfolgen.	Should you require references
Können Sie uns bitte ebenfalls Ihre Geschäftsbedingungen schicken?	We want to point out that
Bitte veranlassen Sie einen Vertreterbesuch in unserer Zentrale.	Delivery should be made by air-freight
Sollten Sie Referenzen benötigen	Could you please also send us your terms of business?
Wir haben in verschiedenen nordeuropäischen Ländern Fabriken.	Please arrange for your representative to visit our head office.

Now write down the underlined German and English expressions.

dankbar	grateful

 **Draft a letter.**

Sie heißen Inge Langer und sind Mitarbeiterin der Firma *Das Rad* in Bremen. Im Auftrag der Firmenleitung sollen Sie Informationen über Telefonanlagen der Firma *Telcom*, 28 Wakefield Street, Sheffield 8VE 17, einholen.

- Teilen Sie mit, dass Ihnen *Telcom* als bekannter Lieferant für Telefonanlagen von Ihrem Geschäftspartner *Euro-Rad* empfohlen wurde.
- Stellen Sie Ihr Unternehmen vor: mittelgroßer deutscher Fahrradhersteller mit Fabriken in verschiedenen nordeuropäischen Ländern.
- Sie sind besonders an den Anlagen von *Telcom* interessiert, da Sie Ihre Fabriken alle mit einem Telefonnetz ausstatten wollen.
- Teilen Sie mit, dass Sie sich daher freuen würden, wenn *Telcom* Ihnen vollständige Informationen über ihr Sortiment von Telefonanlagen schicken könnte.
- Fragen Sie, ob *Telcom* den Einbau ihrer Geräte anbietet.
- Fragen Sie ebenfalls, ob *Telcom* Ihnen ihre Geschäftsbedingungen schicken könnte.
- Bitten Sie darum, dass *Telcom* einen Vertreterbesuch in Ihrer Zentrale in Bremen veranlasst.
- Falls *Telcom* Referenzen benötigen sollte, bitten Sie sie, Kontakt mit dem Bankhaus Neelmeyer in Bremen aufzunehmen.
- Das Bankhaus Neelmeyer freut sich, *Telcom* Auskunft über Ihre Firma zu liefern.
- Sagen Sie, dass Sie hoffen, bald von *Telcom* zu hören.
- Grußformel

 **Here is some help for you.**

comprehensive	umfassend
information on/about	Information über
to install	einbauen
plant	Fabrik, Werk
range of products	Sortiment von Produkten
should you require references	sollten Sie Referenzen benötigen
sb will be pleased	jemand wird sich über etwas freuen
representative	Vertreter
to arrange for s.b. to do s.th.	jemanden veranlassen, etwas zu tun
to be recommended to s.b. by s.b.	jemand wird von jemandem empfohlen
to contact s.b.	Kontakt mit jemandem aufnehmen
to equip	ausstatten
to supply s.b. with s.th.	jdn. mit etwas beliefern, jdm. etwas zur Verfügung stellen
well-known	bekannt

Das Rad GmbH
Breite Straße 12
28325 Bremen
Tel: +49 421 361-18263
Fax: +49 421 361-18264

Ihr Zeichen: Unser Zeichen: Bremen,

35

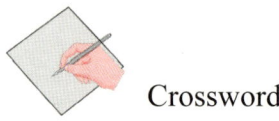 Crossword

1	
2	
3	
4	
5	
6	
7	
8	
9	
10	
11	
12	
13	
14	

Fill in the gaps and complete the crossword.

- *Telcom* (1) _____ a meeting at our (10) ____ Office.

- *Das Rad* and *Euro-Rad* are (2) _____ partners.

- The company wants to (3) _____ all (11) _____ with telephone systems.

- The company gets (13) _____ information on their (5) _____ of products.

- *Telcom* is a (7) ____-_____ (4) _____ of telephone systems.

- They offer to (6) _____ their telephone (9) _____ .

- *Telcom* has been (14) _____ by the embassy.

- The company would like to (8) ____ everything about the (12) terms of _____.

- There is a hidden word in the box. What does it mean? Give a short description.

36

A Telephone Call

Switchboard:	Telecommunication Ltd, good morning. Can I help you?
Paul Gibson:	Yes, could you put me through to the sales department, please?
Switchboard:	Hold the line please, I'll put you through to Mrs Morris now.

Some seconds later …

Debbie Morris:	Sales department, Morris speaking. How can I help you?
Paul Gibson:	Paul Gibson here, good morning. We've had a look at your new *TEL-IN* fax machines at the last Cebit fair and we'd like to place an order. But first we need to know your prices and possible discounts.
Debbie Morris:	The unit price is 500 Euro. As for discounts, they depend on the quantity you want to order.
Paul Gibson:	We need 5.
Debbie Morris:	For orders of 5 or more we can grant you a discount of 10% and an additional cash discount of 3%.
Paul Gibson:	I see. What are your terms of payment and what's the delivery time?
Debbie Morris:	Our terms of payment are settlement within 30 days. We can deliver within 7 days. If you need the goods earlier we can send them by special delivery. But there'll be an extra charge for that.
Paul Gibson:	Thank you for the information. I'll have to discuss that with our purchasing manager. I'll send the order to you by fax later this morning.
Debbie Morris:	Thank you, Mr Gibson. Good bye for now.
Paul Gibson:	Good bye, Mrs Morris.

Questions

a)   What kind of telephone call is the above dialogue?
b)   Who is the caller?
c)   Who gets the call?
d)   What does the caller want?
e)   What information does the caller get?
f)   Will the caller contact Debbie Morris again?
g)   What will the caller have to do before he can place an order?
h)   Which product is the caller interested in?
i)   How many units of the product does the caller need?

What do the people in the dialogue say? Translate into English.

1. Wir können Ihnen einen Rabatt von 10% gewähren.
   _____

2. Der Stückpreis beträgt 10 Euro.
   _____

3. Könnten Sie mich bitte mit der Verkaufsabteilung verbinden?
   _____

4. Wir müssen erst Ihre Preise und eventuellen Rabatte kennen.
   _____

5. Unsere Zahlungsbedingungen sind Zahlung innerhalb 30 Tagen.
   _____

6. Wie ist die Lieferzeit?
   _____

7. Wir würden gerne eine Bestellung aufgeben.
   _____

8. Bleiben Sie dran, ich verbinde Sie.
   _____

9. Was Rabatte betrifft, so hängen die von der Menge ab, die Sie bestellen wollen.
   _____

10. Wir können Ihnen zusätzlich 3% Skonto gewähren.
    _____

11. Was kann ich für Sie tun?
    _____

12. Ich schicke Ihnen die Bestellung heute morgen per Fax.

    _____

13. Wir können innerhalb einer Woche liefern.

    _____

14. Ich muss das mit unserem Einkaufsleiter besprechen.

    _____

15. Wir können die Ware per Eilzustellung schicken.

    _____

Crossword

1
2
3
4
5
6
7
8
9

1 Could you _____ me through to Mr Clayton, please?

2 I will send the _____ to you by mail today.

3 We want to _____ an order.

4 The unit _____ is 100 Euro.

5 How can I _____ you?

6 _____ is the delivery time?

7 _____ the line, please.

8 What _____ I do for you?

9 We can _____ within a week.

Was sagen/schreiben Sie, wenn

a) Sie darum bitten, mit jemandem verbunden zu werden?

    Could you
- [ ] put me up with ..., please?
- [ ] put me into ... please?
- [ ] put me through to ... please?

b) Sie jemanden telefonisch verbinden?

    Hold the
- [ ] phone, please.
- [ ] line, please.
- [ ] connection, please.

c) Sie jemandem einen Rabatt von 15% einräumen können?

    We can grant you
- [ ] 15% discount.
- [ ] a discount of 15%.
- [ ] 15% of a discount.

d) Sie innerhalb einer Woche liefern können?

    We can deliver
- [ ] in week.
- [ ] within week.
- [ ] within a week.

e) Sie eine Bestellung aufgeben möchten?

    We would like to
- [ ] have an order.
- [ ] place an order.
- [ ] put an order.

f) Sie wissen wollen, womit Sie dem Anrufer weiterhelfen können?

    How can I
- [ ] do for you?
- [ ] help you?
- [ ] deal with you?

Have another look at the telephone dialogue you read on page 37.

You will notice that the word '**will**' appears many times. In this case the **future tense** is used.

We use this form when an action will happen at a later date. That later date might just be a few minutes away.

If you use the verb '**will**' you must use **infinitives** afterwards. Follow the formula below!

> **will-future = subject + will + infinitive + phrase**

The examples in the text meant:

(1) The secretary **will put** Mr Gibson through to Mrs Morris.
(2) Telecommunication Ltd **will make** an extra charge, if the customer needs the goods earlier.
(3) Mr Gibson **will have to** confirm the information with the purchasing manager.
(4) Mr Gibson **will send** the order to Mrs Morris by fax.

All four sentences above follow the formula: subject + **will** + **infinitive** + phrase.

Now let us look at the examples from the text.

Find and write down the examples of *will-future* from the dialogue:

1. _____
2. _____
3. _____
4. _____

You can see that all of these sentences follow the same formula!

Let us look at the first sentence you found in the dialogue:

The person at the switchboard now does **a series of things - one *after* the other.**

That person:

a) notes who is on the line [Mr Gibson].
b) notes which department must be contacted [sales department].
c) tries to contact that department.
d) tells Mrs Morris that Mr Gibson is on the line.
e) connects the two.

Persons who work at switchboards know what they must do. To do their job well, they start at (a) and work down the list.

Note: **(e) happens after (a)!** This example explains why the person at the switchboard uses the will-future.

All of the actions happen **later** in a sequence.

Answer the following questions.

(1) What will the person at the switchboard do?
_____

(2) What will Mr Gibson have to discuss with the purchasing manager?
_____

(3) When will Mr Gibson send his fax?
_____

Note: The **German language** often uses the **present tense** for actions in the future, the **English language** uses **will-future.**

Translate into English.

(1) Die Telefonzentrale wird Mr Gibson durchstellen.

_____

(2) „Bleiben Sie bitte dran; Ich stelle Sie durch."

_____

(3) Ich werde es besprechen müssen./Ich muss es besprechen.

_____

(4) Was wird Herr Gibson besprechen müssen?

_____

Note: *will* is **not** the German *wollen*!

'I **will** go' „Ich **will gehen**"
heißt: heißt:
„ich **werde gehen**," 'I **want to go**'
nicht **oder**
„ich will gehen"! 'I **would like to go**'.

So, remember:

You say → I want an ice-cream! Ich will ein Eis! ← *You think*

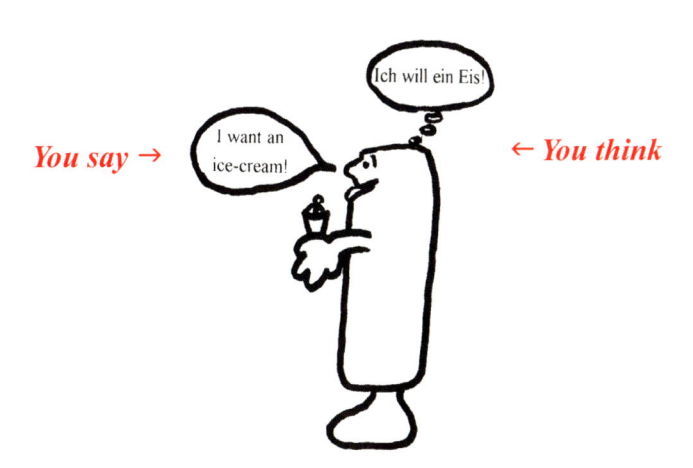

Translate into English.

(1) Ich will/möchte eine Tasse Tee.

(2) Er schreibt bald.

(3) Ich stelle Sie durch.

(4) Er will die Hannover Messe besuchen.

(5) Ich bespreche es mit dem Projektmanager.

(6) Ich muss es mit dem Projektmanager besprechen.

(7) Der Chef will keine Änderung sehen.

(8) Wir rufen Sie am nächsten Mittwoch zurück.

(9) Die Preise bleiben bis zum Jahresende gleich.

(10) Ich bedaure, aber das wird nicht möglich sein.

Now try a few sentences the other way round.

(1) I will see to it at once.
_____

(2) I will pay in cash.
_____

(3) (The telephone is ringing:) " I'll answer it. "
_____

(4) I will come to your party.
_____

(5) I want to speak to the project manager.
_____

(6) The customer wants to pay for the goods by cheque.
_____

(7) He doesn't want to pay so much.
_____

(8) We will call you back.
_____

(9) He wants to buy a new car.
_____

(10) I will wish him 'Merry Christmas' when I see him.
_____

Crossword

Now you should be able to fill in this crossword without any difficulties. Almost all of the words are taken from the chapter you have just completed.

Across

- 1 A: Werbung, Anzeige
- 1 O: Anfrage
- 3 A: Datum
- 3 H: bestätigen
- 4 O: neuester, letzter
- 6 A: hinein
- 6 I: Referenz (Kurzform)
- 7 O: Ausgabe (von Zeitung)
- 9 N: Menge
- 10 A: Lautsprecher
- 11 O: bestellen, Bestellung
- 12 C: beträchtlich
- 13 Q: (sich) beziehen (auf)
- 14 A: Spitze, Oberteil, oben
- 14 J: Zukunft
- 15 C: Preis (Mz.)
- 16 K: Ende
- 16 O: hören (Gerundium)
- 19 C: Satz, Rate, Kurs (Mz.)
- 20 I: Rabatt
- 21 E: in
- 21 P: mittel
- 22 G: Auto (Mz.)
- 23 A: echt, real
- 24 N: komplett, total
- 25 C: speziell, besonders
- 27 K: Entwicklung
- 29 A: Lied
- 29 F: dankbar
- 29 O: Adresse
- 32 A: (Preise) nennen, zitieren
- 32 J: etabliert, eingeführt
- 34 E: bald
- 34 O: aktuell
- 35 A: bezahlen
- 37 E: spielen
- 37 J: Hersteller
- 38 A: nicht
- 39 F: Anlage (in Brief) (Kurzform)
- 39 L: Referenz (Mz.)

Down

- 1 A: zusätzlich
- 1 C: Mehrwertsteuer (Kurzwort)
- 1 F: heute
- 1 J: Manager
- 1 M: (Zahlungs-)Bedingungen
- 1 Q: (Preis-)Angebot
- 1 T: ausruhen, Rest
- 6 T: nein
- 7 G: kürzlich, jüngst
- 8 C: du
- 8 K: Möbel
- 9 R: deshalb
- 12 A: innerhalb
- 12 C: Lieferant
- 13 T: gleich, sogar
- 15 H: (Verkehrs-)Zeichen, unterschreiben
- 15 P: Abteilung
- 16 L: bemerken, wahrnehmen, Mitteilung
- 16 U: gehen
- 17 E: Detail, Einzelheit
- 18 J: Messe (Mz.)
- 19 N: Qualität
- 19 U: Komponente, Bestandteil
- 20 S: mit
- 22 A: Zweigstelle (Mz.)
- 23 D: führend
- 23 F: Katalog
- 23 K: (Markt-)Stand
- 27 I: interessiert
- 27 O: führen, anführen
- 29 R: Rose
- 31 A: Ausrüstung
- 32 C: nur
- 32 M: Broschüre, Prospekt
- 32 O: erhöht werden, zunehmen
- 32 U: Brief
- 33 G: für
- 34 E: Muster
- 38 C: zu

Crossword

Useful phrases: Enquiries

Opening

We	refer to	our visit	to your stand	at the recent fair in London
		your advertisement	in this week's edition of	*Frankfurter Rundschau*
	have seen	your advertisement	on the Internet	
		your home page		

Background

We	are a	well-established	retailer	of		clothes
		medium-sized	wholesaler			furniture
		leading	supplier			bicycles
		well-known	manufacturer			etc.
			producer			
			retail chain	with	branches	all over Germany
			company		plants	in European countries
					etc.	
	want to	develop wider sources of supply				
	are	particularly	interested in	the	computers	that you offer
		especially			dynamos	
					bicycles	
					etc.	

Why are we writing?

| As | the market | for | computers | is increasing | enormously | we are looking | for | new |
| | | | | | rapidly | | | |

suppliers

We are	interested in	your	systems	because	we	would like to	equip	our office
			products			want to		
			etc.					

48

What do we want?   (Request)

We would	therefore	be	grateful pleased thankful	if you could if you would	quote us	your	lowest	prices	☆
					send us let us have		current latest	catalogue price list brochure	
							information	on	your ⚙

☆	for	loudspeakers soundcards etc.
⚙	range	of	telephone systems etc.

What else do we want? (Additional Request)

Please		let us also have	details of your			terms retail discounts	
Could you	please		samples of your products			for testing	
		arrange for	your representative	to visit us	at our	head office London office	

Further phrases

If your	prices discounts	meet our	requirements expectations	we	will be	willing happy	to place	substantial further

_____ orders with you

Should you	require want	references	please contact	Bankhaus Neelmeyer Barclay's Bank	in	Bremen London

Closing

We	look forward to	hearing from you	in the near future
	hope to	hear from you	soon in due course

7 Gosch, Overbeck-Hellwing, Besch - ISBN 978-3-8120-0847-1

UNIT THREE: OFFERS

Let us start with a definition: An offer is a statement from a company that it is willing to sell

- certain goods and services
- on certain terms, at
- certain prices.

Usually companies make **offers** after customers have made enquiries. Answers to special enquiries are called **quotations** – remember, the verb we use is: **'to quote'** a price!

If you are responding to an enquiry, then write this in your letter e.g. *We refer to your enquiry of …. [date] asking for information on our products.*

Remember, you want the customer to buy your goods, so take the chance to present your new products, or to advertise the goods you want to sell, e.g. *As a leading manufacturer of sportswear, we produce a wide range of exclusive casual clothes, made from only natural materials.*

If you have new leaflets, supply them with the catalogues and let your customers know, e.g. *May we draw your attention to our special offer indicated in the leaflet.*

Now that you know the background, you can write your letters. Check exactly what the customer wants to know and then answer all questions about:

- **prices** e.g. *Our prices are quoted ex works and include packing.*

- **additional charges** e.g. *An additional charge is only made for express delivery.*

- **discounts** e.g. *We will be willing to allow you a trade discount of 5% on orders worth at least €5,000.*

- **terms of payment** e.g. *Our terms of payment for first orders are* **documents against payment.** *We request payment by confirmed and irrevocable letter of credit.*

- **terms of delivery** e.g. *Delivery will be made within 2 weeks after receipt of order. Shipment can be arranged immediately after receipt of order.*

You can send the customer a **non-binding** offer or make a **firm offer. Firm** means the same as concrete, confirmed and guaranteed. The prices will not change within a certain period of time.

A **non-binding offer** means: the seller might change the prices between the time of making the offer and receiving the order. This might be because of changes in the price of raw materials etc

Mark the following points as *true* or *false*.

	true	false
1. An offer is a statement of intent to sell goods or services.	☐	☐
2. If you don't supply the goods, you should not answer a letter of enquiry.	☐	☐
3. An offer must include details of **delivery.**	☐	☐
4. You should never include leaflets and new details in an offer.	☐	☐
5. Terms of payment are always included in an offer.	☐	☐
6. Never tell your customer when delivery can be expected.	☐	☐
7. An enquiry is a chance for your company to win further customers.	☐	☐
8. Prices will change if the offer is **firm.**	☐	☐
9. If the price of your raw materials changes, you should make a **firm offer.**	☐	☐
10. You should include details of **prices** and **additional charges** in your offer.	☐	☐

Now summarize what you know about offers.

_____
_____
_____
_____
_____
_____
_____
_____
_____
_____

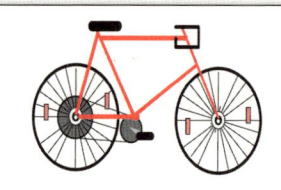

Mr J. Clease
The Bike Shop
27 Brompton Road
LONDON SW 11
ENGLAND

Das Rad GmbH
Breite Straße 12
28325 Bremen
Tel: +49 421 361-18263
Fax: +49 421 361-18264

Your ref: JC/dm
Our ref: PvZ/dl
Date:

Dear Mr Clease

Your enquiry dated …

Thank you for your enquiry of … (see date of enquiry).

Please find enclosed our latest catalogue, price list and terms of business.

The prices quoted are FOB Bremen and shipment can be arranged immediately after receipt of order.

We can grant retail discounts of 15% on the net price and we are willing to let you have a further first order discount of 5%.

As we have not done business before, we request payment by irrevocable and confirmed letter of credit.

We hope that our prices and terms meet with your approval and that you will decide to place your order with us.

Yours sincerely
Das Rad GmbH

Patrick von Zahn
Sales Manager
Encs: catalogue, price list, terms of business

Questions

a) What does this letter refer to?
b) What does the sender say about prices?
c) What is enclosed with the letter?
d) When can delivery be arranged?
e) What discounts are offered?
f) How should payment be effected?

Look at the letter from „Das Rad" again. You will see that prices are quoted **FOB Bremen.** FOB is an Incoterm and means **F**ree **o**n **B**oard.

Incoterms are conditions of delivery. If prices are quoted **FOB** the seller pays all costs until the goods cross the ship's railing. After this point the buyer covers all costs: Insurance, transport and unloading.

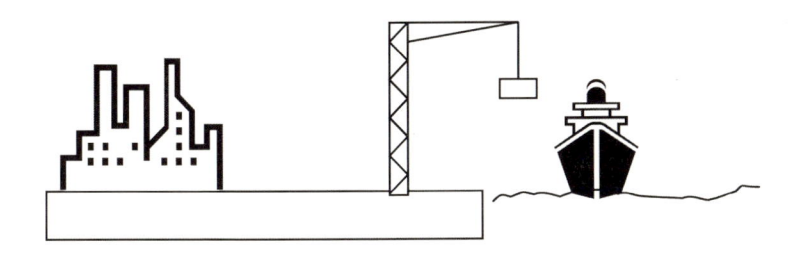

Crossword

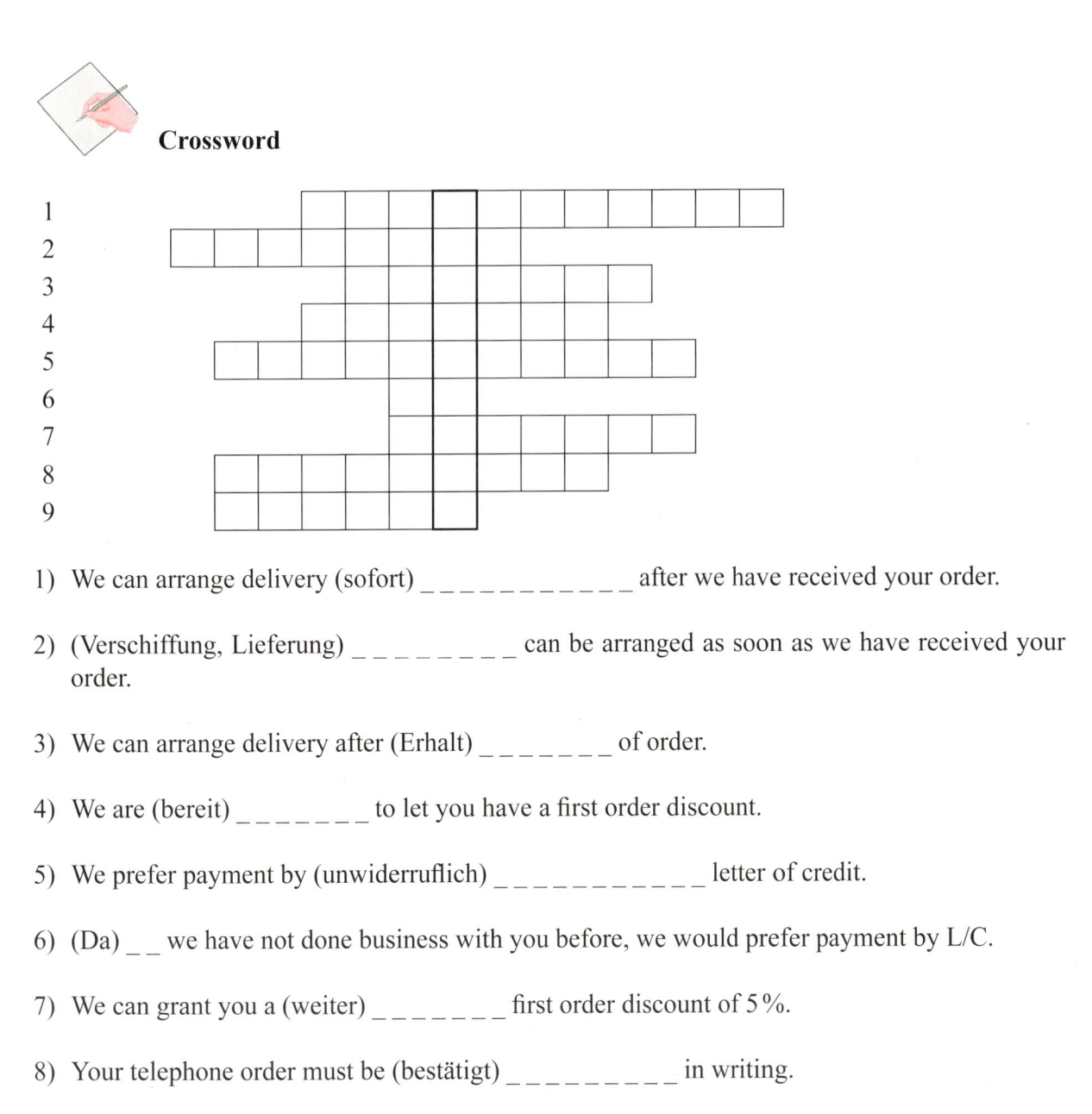

1) We can arrange delivery (sofort) _ _ _ _ _ _ _ _ _ _ _ after we have received your order.

2) (Verschiffung, Lieferung) _ _ _ _ _ _ _ _ can be arranged as soon as we have received your order.

3) We can arrange delivery after (Erhalt) _ _ _ _ _ _ _ of order.

4) We are (bereit) _ _ _ _ _ _ _ to let you have a first order discount.

5) We prefer payment by (unwiderruflich) _ _ _ _ _ _ _ _ _ _ letter of credit.

6) (Da) _ _ we have not done business with you before, we would prefer payment by L/C.

7) We can grant you a (weiter) _ _ _ _ _ _ _ first order discount of 5 %.

8) Your telephone order must be (bestätigt) _ _ _ _ _ _ _ _ _ in writing.

9) We will (entscheiden) _ _ _ _ _ _ later, if we want to place an order.

53

Was sagen/schreiben Sie, wenn

a) Sie sich für die Anfrage vom 2. November 20 .. bedanken wollen?

b) die angegebenen Preise FOB Bremen sind?

c) Sie einen zusätzlichen Rabatt gewähren können?

d) Sie Bezahlung durch unwiderrufliches Akkreditiv erbitten?

e) Sie hoffen, dass Ihre Preise die Zustimmung Ihres Geschäftspartners finden?

f) Sie die Lieferung sofort nach Auftragseingang veranlassen können?

g) Sie bereit sind, einen Rabatt zu gewähren?

h) Sie hoffen, dass Ihre Geschäftspartner bei Ihnen bestellen?

i) Sie in der Anlage den neuesten Katalog übersenden?

A Letter of Credit is the most common way of payment in foreign trade:

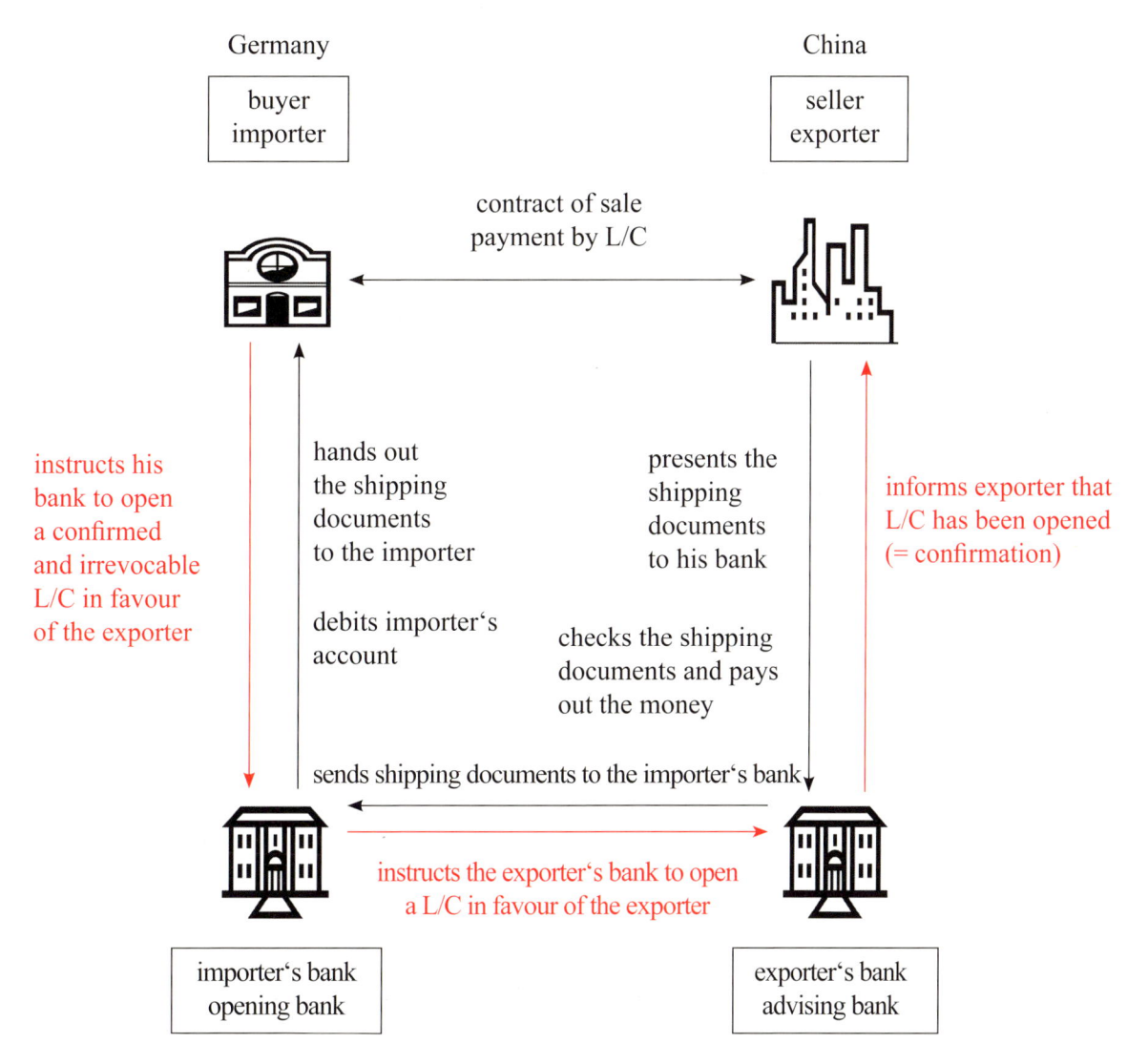

Germany	China
buyer / importer	seller / exporter

contract of sale
payment by L/C

Germany side (buyer/importer → importer's bank):
- instructs his bank to open a confirmed and irrevocable L/C in favour of the exporter
- hands out the shipping documents to the importer
- debits importer's account

China side (exporter ↔ exporter's bank):
- presents the shipping documents to his bank
- informs exporter that L/C has been opened (= confirmation)
- checks the shipping documents and pays out the money

sends shipping documents to the importer's bank

instructs the exporter's bank to open a L/C in favour of the exporter

importer's bank	exporter's bank
opening bank	advising bank

This L/C is **confirmed,** i.e. the exporter's bank confirms that the exporter will get the money from them.

This L/C is **irrevocable,** i.e. the importer cannot withdraw his instructions to the bank.

Some information on discounts:

Retail discount — This discount is granted to retailers by wholesalers or manufacturers.

First order discount — This discount is granted to a buyer when he places his first order with a company.

Draft a letter.

Sie heißen Zhang Jin und arbeiten bei der Firma *Lung Mingh Ltd.* Schreiben Sie ein Angebot an die Firma *Das Rad*.

- Bedanken Sie sich für die Anfrage vom … (siehe *enquiry*).
- In der Anlage übersenden Sie die neueste Broschüre und Ihre Geschäftsbedingungen.
- Sie werden den gewünschten Musterdynamo mit getrennter Post übersenden.
- Teilen Sie mit, dass Sie bereit sind, einen Händlerrabatt von 5 % für Bestellungen im Wert von 10.000,00 € oder mehr zu gewähren.
- Bei Erstbestellungen sind die Zahlungsbedingungen Dokumente gegen Kasse.
- Sie sind sicher, dass die Qualität Ihrer Dynamos den Anforderungen von *Das Rad* entspricht, und dass *Das Rad* gerne bei Ihnen bestellen wird.
- Sollte *Das Rad* irgendwelche Fragen haben oder weitere Informationen benötigen, soll die Firma *Das Rad* nicht zögern, sich mit Ihnen in Verbindung zu setzen.

Here is some help for you.

der gewünschte Musterdynamo	mit getrennter Post
the sample dynamo you requested	*under separate cover*

wir sind bereit	Bestellungen im Wert von … € oder mehr
we are willing	*orders worth … € or more*

den Anforderungen entsprechen	zögern
to meet the requirements	*to hesitate*

Dokumente gegen Kasse
Documents against payment

Lung Mingh Ltd 23 Xingh Mu Beijing Republic of China   Telephone: 008610 543764   Fax: 008610 543765

Your ref:
Our ref:
Date:

There are eight hidden words or phrases in this wordsquare.

a	p	p	l	o	n	t	i	v	o	n	t	u	e	l	l	y	n	q	e	r	u
b	n	l	c	g	h	s	t	i	e	r	g	m	e	n	t	z	z	r	t	n	
m	m	e	e	t	y	o	u	r	r	e	q	u	i	r	e	m	e	n	t	s	d
o	h	k	f	a	d	t	r	r	e	l	i	t	m	o	b	e	r	m	e	m	e
d	c	o	f	e	s	t	c	o	n	t	a	c	t	f	r	i	k	b	o	p	r
d	e	r	m	t	r	e	e	w	s	u	z	u	m	i	n	g	t	r	i	l	s
e	r	n	i	n	g	w	f	e	t	z	h	t	u	i	k	l	w	i	i	s	e
r	h	w	o	a	r	e	w	i	l	l	i	n	g	h	d	e	t	o	b	u	p
s	g	e	r	m	a	t	i	c	n	s	t	q	u	r	a	t	i	u	n	l	a
w	o	r	g	r	t	i	k	l	a	d	f	t	r	u	z	n	j	n	r	i	r
o	d	o	n	h	e	s	i	t	a	t	e	t	r	e	w	t	r	g	s	s	a
r	s	g	t	h	g	u	i	p	a	f	g	n	r	t	e	q	e	h	z	t	t
t	w	i	e	s	t	e	r	b	a	l	d	m	c	w	z	w	i	k	u	n	e
h	r	e	i	k	l	v	h	d	s	q	e	g	n	l	e	h	t	a	q	u	c
s	e	f	t	l	a	n	k	r	e	t	z	u	m	i	o	n	g	h	e	t	o
r	z	t	i	o	m	i	n	g	s	t	i	l	s	b	u	s	f	o	t	e	v
a	g	r	h	z	u	m	f	d	h	d	e	h	s	q	d	v	e	l	t	e	e
g	z	u	i	b	d	e	k	l	e	w	r	t	h	u	n	e	q	d	t	w	r
t	h	e	d	y	n	a	m	o	s	y	o	u	r	e	q	u	e	s	t	e	d

a) In der Anlage übersenden wir ...   e) im Wert (von)
b) zögern   f) Ihren Anforderungen entsprechen
c) die gewünschten Dynamos   g) (wir) sind bereit
d) mit getrennter Post   h) kontaktieren

Fill in the gaps with suitable words taken from the wordsquare.

1. _____ our latest catalogue.

2. Do not _____ to contact us.

3. We _____ to let you have a first order discount of 5%.

4. We grant a discount of 5% for orders _____ 10,000.00 € or more.

5. We are sending the samples _____ .

6. We will send _____ as soon as possible.

7. We are sure that our products will _____ .

8. Do not hesitate to _____ us.

Some important information on foreign trade:

- The owner of the shipping documents is the owner of the consignment/goods.
- You need the shipping documents to prove that you are the owner of the consignment/goods.
- The owner of the shipping documents is allowed to collect the consignment/goods from the port or from the airport.
- The moment the seller hands over the shipping documents to the buyer or his middleman/agent/bank, he has to be absolutely sure that he will get his money.

Ways of payment in foreign trade

Documents against payment (D/P) or Cash against documents (CAD)

The shipping documents are only given to the buyer against payment of the seller's invoice or against payment of a draft drawn on the buyer by the seller.

Some more information on discounts:

Trade discount   This discount is granted, if the business partners are dealers or if one partner is a middleman.

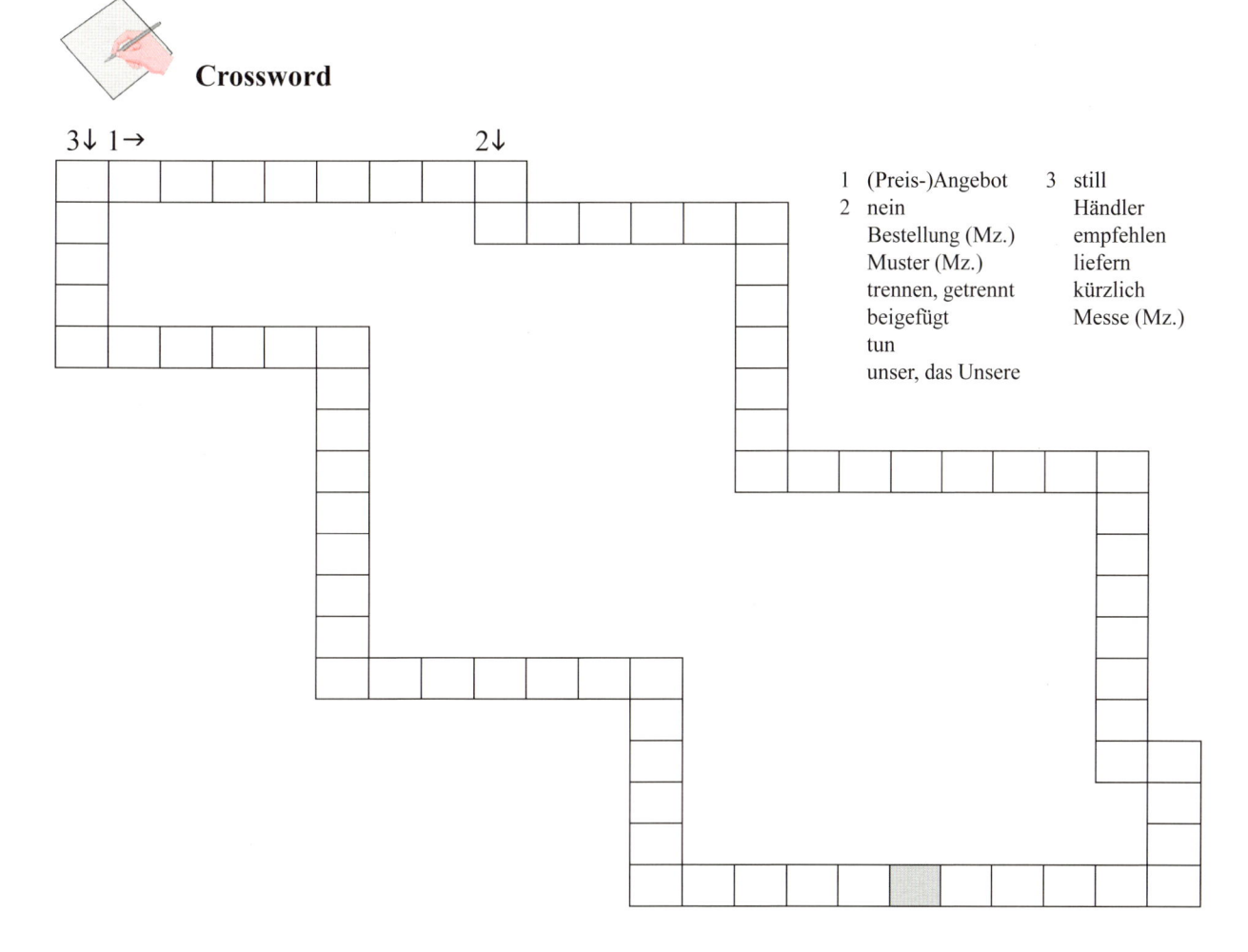

Crossword

3↓ 1→   2↓

1 (Preis-)Angebot	3 still
2 nein	Händler
Bestellung (Mz.)	empfehlen
Muster (Mz.)	liefern
trennen, getrennt	kürzlich
beigefügt	Messe (Mz.)
tun	
unser, das Unsere	

59

Language Practice

If you want to write good business letters, you must understand **and use** the passive voice.
We use the **passive voice** to stress what happens to the object. Only sometimes do we mention who does the action, e.g. *This letter was typed by my secretary* (by-agent).
You all know the phrase: *Made in Germany* This is the short form of the passive sentence: ***This product was made in Germany.***
In this case it is **not** important to know who made the product. So you do not need to mention the ***by-agent.***

Now let us look at an example:

(a) *'We send all our products FOB-Bremen'.*
(b) *'All our products are sent FOB-Bremen'.*

Sentence (a) is active, and sentence (b) is passive.

Let us have a look at the parts of the two sentences.

	Who is the subject?	What is the verb/action?	What is the object?
SENTENCE (a)			

SENTENCE (b)			

As you can see the **object** of sentence (a) becomes the **subject** of sentence (b).

Remember, verbs have 3 forms.
For the **passive voice** we use **3rd form**
e.g.

irregular verb	(to) do	did	**done**
	(to) see	saw	**seen**
regular verb	(to) refer	referred	**referred**
	(to) talk	talked	**talked**

How do we form a passive voice sentence?

Write down the 3 steps you took to get from sentence (a) to sentence (b).

(1) _____

(2) _____

(3) _____

Your work should now look like this:

(1) The **object phrase** = *all our products* = subject of the new <u>passive</u> sentence.
    Start your sentence with this **new subject.**

(2) *'Products' = They = 3rd person plural.*
    What **form of the helping verb** 'to be' fits this person? _____

(3) The verb/action = *to send.*
    What is the **3rd form** of this verb? _____

All you did was put the parts together: ***All our products are sent FOB-Bremen.***

Use the following formula to help you.

> **New subject   +   helping verb   +   3rd form of verb/action**

We often use **modal verbs** in passive sentences; verbs like *must, can, will* etc.
In this case, we use the following formula:

> **New subject   +   modal verb   +   be   +   3rd form of verb/action**

Let us look at some examples from the letters.

We can arrange delivery immediately.
   Delivery **can be arranged** immediately.

You should effect payment by irrevocable and confirmed letter of credit.
   Payment **should be effected** by irrevocable and confirmed letter of credit.

We will grant you a further first order discount of 5%
   A further first order discount of 5% **will be granted.**

We cannot offer installation of our systems.
   Installation (of our systems) **cannot be offered.**

Change the following sentences from the active voice into the passive voice and decide whether you need to mention the *by-agent*.

(1) Our company doesn't make dynamos.
_____

(2) Our company manufactures all parts.
_____

(3) A Chinese company made the dynamos.
_____

(4) *Mighty Logistics* sent the goods by air-freight.
_____

(5) We have contacted our suppliers.
_____

(6) Our manager has made an enquiry.
_____

(7) We will deliver the goods within 3 weeks.
_____

(8) You must make your special requests in writing.
_____

(9) We can arrange special delivery.
_____

(10) You should make payment as soon as possible.
_____

Now try it the other way round.

(1) The goods haven't been delivered yet.

(2) Payment has been effected by irrevocable and confirmed letter of credit.

(3) The dynamos you requested will be sent under separate cover.

(4) Our offices will be equipped with a new telephone system.

(5) We were offered installation of the new system by *T&H*.

Translate the following sentences into English.

(1) (Die Firma) *T&H* wurde uns von (der Firma) *Telcom* empfohlen.

(2) Die Lieferung wird sofort nach Erhalt der Bestellung erfolgen.

(3) Die Waren wurden gestern geliefert.

(4) Ein Erstbestellungsrabatt von 5% wird gewährt.

Draft a letter by putting the phrases from the chart into the correct order

Sie heißen Gabriela Zastrow und arbeiten bei der Firma *Sport + Spaß* in Bremen. Sie beantworten die Anfrage der Firma *Sportmexx*, der Sie notwendige Informationen entnehmen.

- Beziehen Sie sich auf die Anfrage vom ... (siehe *enquiry*), in der die Firma *Sportmexx* um Informationen über Ihre Produkte bittet.
- Sie waren erfreut zu lesen, dass die Firma *Sportmexx* an der Sportkleidung interessiert ist, die Sie auf der Messe *Sport and Leisure* in Birmingham präsentiert haben.
- In der Anlage übersenden Sie Ihren aktuellen Katalog und Preisliste zusammen mit einem Auftragsformular.
- Sie möchten darauf hinweisen, dass Sie ein Sortiment exklusiver hochwertiger Freizeitkleidung anbieten, das aus natürlichen Rohmaterialien hergestellt wird.
- Wie gewünscht, werden Sie eine Musterauswahl Ihrer Sportbekleidung mit getrennter Post schicken.
- Sie möchten *Sportmexx* auf Ihr Sonderangebot über Tennisbekleidung aufmerksam machen.
- Ihre Preise sind ab Werk angegeben, einschließlich Verpackung.
- Sie sind gewillt, *Sportmexx* einen Händlerrabatt von 5% auf Aufträge im Wert von mindestens 5.000,00 € einzuräumen.
- Sie bitten um Zahlung durch bestätigtes unwiderrufliches Akkreditiv.
- Die Lieferung wird innerhalb von 2 Wochen nach Auftragseingang erfolgen.
- Sie freuen sich darauf, mit der Firma *Sportmexx* in nächster Zeit Geschäfte zu tätigen.
- Grußformel

	We request payment by confirmed and irrevocable letter of credit.
	Please find enclosed our latest catalogue and price list together with an order form.
	Delivery will be made within two weeks after receipt of order.
	We refer to your enquiry of ... (*date*), asking for information on our products.
	We look forward to doing business with you in the near future.
	Our prices are quoted ex works and include packing.
	Yours sincerely
	We want to point out that we offer a range of exclusive high-quality casual clothes made of natural raw materials.
	We are willing to let you have a trade discount of 5% on orders worth at least 5,000.00 €.
	We were pleased to read that you are interested in our sportswear presented at the trade fair *Sport and Leisure* in Birmingham.
	As requested, we will send a collection of samples of our sportswear under separate cover.
	May we draw your attention to our special offer for tennis sportswear.

Sport + Spaß

Walliser Str. 125
28325 Bremen

Tel: 0421 361-2728
Fax: 0421 361-2245

Ihre Zeichen   Unsere Zeichen   Bremen,_____

_____
_____
_____
_____
_____
_____
_____
_____
_____
_____
_____
_____
_____
_____
_____
_____
_____
_____
_____
_____
_____

Sport + Spaß

Walliser Straße 125
28325 Bremen
Tel: 0421 361-2728 – Fax: 0421 361-2245

AUFTRAGSFORMULAR

Auftragsnummer:			Kundennummer:	Datum	
Pos.Nr.	Anzahl	Artikelnr.	Artikelbezeichnung	Preis	

Translate the following sentences and fill in the crossword below.

1. Wir bitten um Zahlung durch **bestätigtes** unwiderrufliches Akkreditiv.
   _____

2. Wir werden Ihnen **Muster** mit getrennter Post schicken.
   _____

3. Unsere Preise sind *ab Werk* **angegeben.**
   _____

4. Unsere Preise **beinhalten/sind einschließlich** Verpackung.
   _____

5. Unsere Sportbekleidung ist ein **Sonderangebot.**
   _____

6. Wir stellen exklusive **Sportbekleidung** her.
   _____

7. Wieviel sind die Trainingsanzüge (track suits) **wert?**
   _____

Crossword

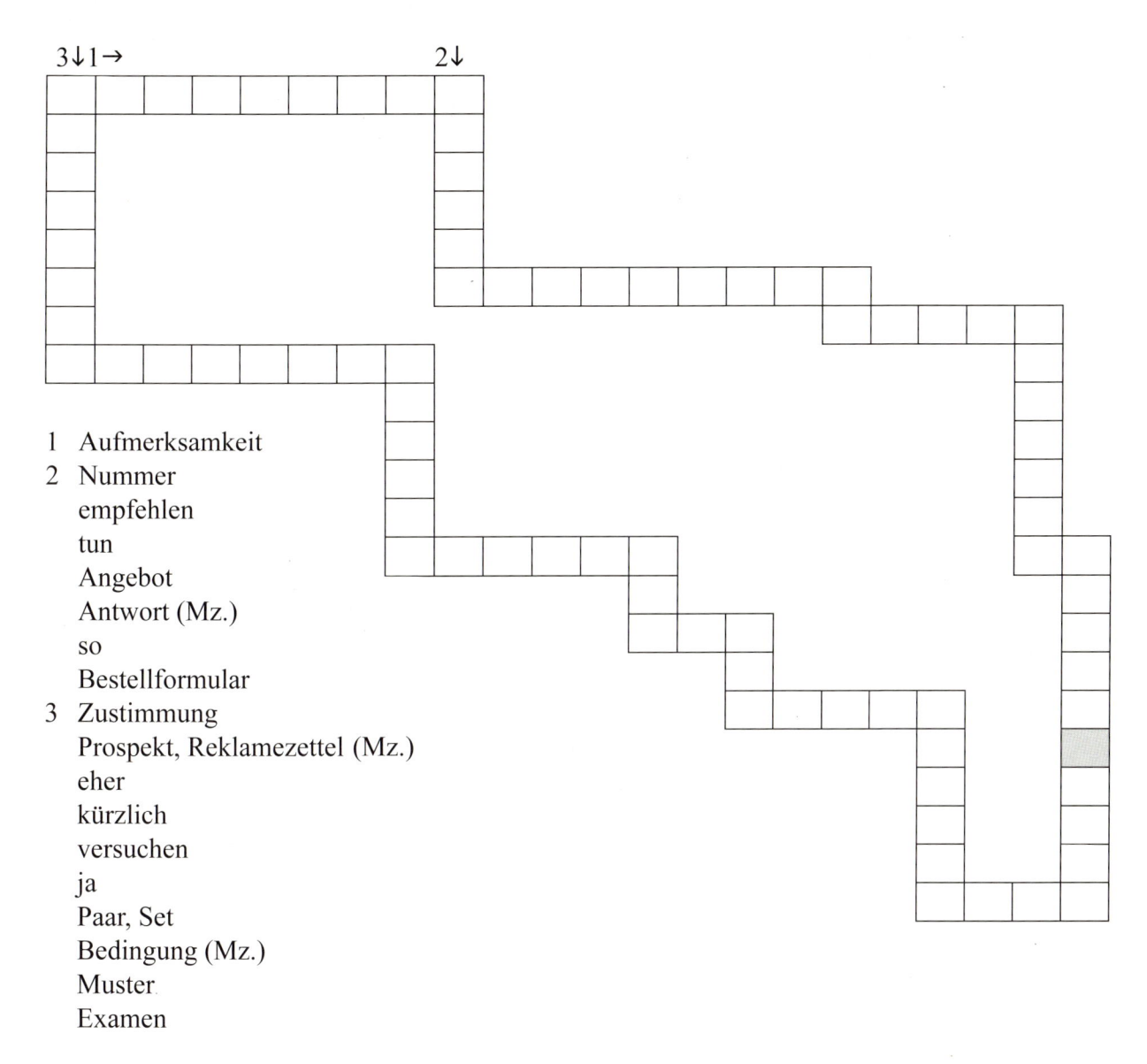

3↓ 1→   2↓

1 Aufmerksamkeit
2 Nummer
　empfehlen
　tun
　Angebot
　Antwort (Mz.)
　so
　Bestellformular
3 Zustimmung
　Prospekt, Reklamezettel (Mz.)
　eher
　kürzlich
　versuchen
　ja
　Paar, Set
　Bedingung (Mz.)
　Muster
　Examen

In this letter the prices are quoted **Ex Works. Ex Works** is another **Incoterm.** If prices are quoted **Ex Works,** the buyer receives the goods at the seller's premises. The buyer has to pay all costs for transport and insurance from the seller's premises to his plant or office.

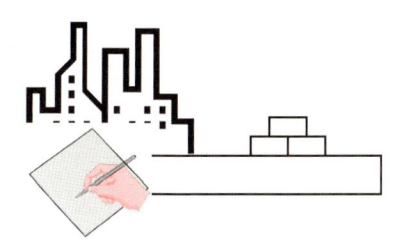

Draft a letter.

Sie sind Alec Simon von der Firma *CompaTec* und schreiben ein Angebot an die Firma *Vobas*. Adresse und Ansprechpartner bei *Vobas* entnehmen Sie der Anfrage von *Vobas*.

- Beziehen Sie sich auf die Anfrage vom ... (siehe *enquiry*).
- Sie waren erfreut zu lesen, dass Vobas an den im Internet angebotenen Computerbauteilen interessiert ist.
- Sie sind ein bekannter Hersteller von hochwertigen Computerbauteilen in England mit weltweiten Geschäftsverbindungen.
- Sie sind erfreut, ein Preisangebot für folgende Waren zu übermitteln:
- 1.000 Soundkarten   38,50 € pro Stück
- 1.500 Lautsprecher   30,00 € pro Paar (per Set)
- Sie sind bereit, einen Erstauftragsrabatt von 3 % und einen weiteren Mengenrabatt von 5 % für Bestellungen ab 1.000 Stück zu gewähren.
- Ihre Preise sind DDP Bremen angegeben.
- Die Lieferung erfolgt normalerweise per Schiff. Sollte *Vobas* Lieferung per Luftfracht wünschen, ergibt sich eine Zusatzgebühr von 83,00 €.
- Die Zahlung sollte per *Dokumente gegen Kasse* erfolgen.
- In der Anlage übersenden Sie die Geschäftsbedingungen.
- Dieses Angebot ist fest für einen Zeitraum von vier Wochen.
- Sollte *Vobas* weitere Fragen haben oder irgendwelche Informationen benötigen, soll *Vobas* nicht zögern, sich mit Ihnen in Verbindung zu setzen.
- Grußformel

In this letter the prices are quoted **DDP Bremen. DDP** is another **incoterm** and means **D**elivered **D**uty **P**aid. If prices are quoted **DDP** the seller pays all costs until the goods have reached the buyer's plant or office.

CompaTec

35 Moseley Street
London SW 1
Tel. 01-4674358
Fax: 01-4684359
E-mail: Compatec@britcom.co.uk

Your ref:
Our ref:
Date:

Choose the right definition and match it with the correct translation.

1 trade discount	a supermarket where only traders buy b discount only traders get c discount only granted at trade fairs	1 Bitte, Wunsch
2 irrevocable	a stupid new word b Irishman who is able to work c s.th. that cannot be changed or altered	2 Vertreter
3 under separate cover	a lovers who do not live together are *under separate cover* b James Bond on a very secret mission c not in the same envelope	3 Prospekt, Reklamezettel
4 hesitate	a French for *his head* b to pause or wait c short for *his evil deed*	4 angeben, bezeichnen
5 representative	a present that is given back b short for *recent activity* c an agent of a firm	5 unwiderruflich
6 indicate	a house of an Indian b Indiana Jones' credit card c to show or to tell	6 (Preis-)Angebot
7 terms of payment	a conditions relating to doing business b any of the four terms of a year when companies pay their suppliers c accepting that you must pay	7 Antwort
8 leaflet	a leaves that are left lying on the ground (especially in autumn) b printed sheet of paper containing information c short for *leave my house and let me be*	8 Händlerrabatt
9 reply	a another word for *answer* b s.b.'s second flop c lie a reporter tells	9 Zahlungs-bedingungen
10 non-binding	a loose friendship b s.th. that is not thrown into the bin c opposite of *firm, concrete*	10 zögern
11 quotation	a opposite of *rotation* b the price that sb says they would charge for a piece of work or goods c Latin for *where is the station?*	11 freibleibend
12 request	a name of a soap opera b act of politely asking for s.th. c short for *could you please repeat the last question?*	12 mit getrennter Post

Now write down the words from the previous exercise with their definitions and translations.

Word	Definition	Translation
1		
2		
3		
4		
5		
6		
7		
8		
9		
10		
11		
12		

Fill in the table with suitable verbs and nouns.

Nouns	Verbs	Nouns	Verbs
advertisement			to produce
trade			to know
enclosure			to sell
pleasure			to inform
decision			to hesitate

Now fill in the gaps with suitable words from the list above.

1. We are interested in the soundcards that you _____ on the Internet.

2. We _____ our latest catalogue.

3. Our company policy is always _____ our customers.

4. We do not _____ in this line of business any more.

5. We hope you will _____ to place your business with us.

6. Please let us have _____ about your new computer equipment.

7. We are well-known for our high-quality _____.

8. We _____ computers.

9. Our _____ of market trends is excellent.

10. We will supply the goods without _____.

Was sagen/schreiben Sie, wenn

a) Sie bedauern, mitteilen zu müssen, dass …?

    We
- ☐ refer to inform you that …
- ☐ require to inform you that …
- ☐ regret to inform you that …

b) Sie darauf hinweisen wollen, dass …?

    We want to
- ☐ point at that …
- ☐ point out that …
- ☐ point to that …

c) Sie bereit sind, Rabatt zu gewähren?

    We are
- ☐ willing to grant a discount.
- ☐ waiting to grant a discount.
- ☐ writing to grant a discount.

d) Sie mitteilen wollen, dass die Lieferung innerhalb von 4 Wochen erfolgen kann?

    Delivery
- ☐ will be arranged within 4 weeks.
- ☐ would be arranged within 4 weeks.
- ☐ can be arranged within 4 weeks.

e) Sie hoffen, dass Ihr Angebot den Erwartungen der anderen Firma entspricht?

    We hope that our offer meets your
- ☐ requests.
- ☐ expectations.
- ☐ requirements.

f) Sie sich darauf freuen, mit der anderen Firma Geschäfte zu machen?

    We look forward to
- ☐ making business with you.
- ☐ having business with you.
- ☐ doing business with you.

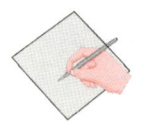

Draft a letter.

Sie heißen Fred Murray und sind Mitarbeiter der Firma **Telcom.** Sie beantworten die Anfrage der Firma **Das Rad.**

- Sie bedanken sich für die Anfrage der Firma *Das Rad* vom … (siehe *enquiry*).
- In der Anlage übersenden Sie den aktuellen Katalog und die Preisliste.
- Weisen Sie darauf hin, dass Sie nur anspruchsvolle Geräte produzieren, die den Erfordernissen der europäischen Sicherheitsvorschriften entsprechen.
- Sie bedauern, dass Sie nicht den Einbau der Geräte anbieten können, Sie können jedoch Ihren Geschäftspartner *Technik & Hilfe* empfehlen.
- In der Anlage übersenden Sie ebenfalls die Geschäftsbedingungen.
- Die Preise gelten ab Werk.
- Sie sind bereit, einen Mengenrabatt von 2% zu gewähren für Aufträge über 100 Stück.
- Sie teilen mit, dass die Lieferung innerhalb von 4 Wochen nach Auftragsbestätigung veranlasst werden kann.
- Die Waren sind in seefesten Kisten verpackt.
- Ihre Zahlungsbedingungen sind: 30 Tage nach Erhalt der Waren, für Zahlung innerhalb von 10 Tagen gewähren Sie 2% Skonto.
- Wie gewünscht wird Ihr Vertreter mit *Das Rad* innerhalb dieses Monats Kontakt aufnehmen.
- Sie hoffen, dass Ihr Angebot den Erwartungen von Das Rad entspricht und freuen sich darauf mit *das Rad* in naher Zukunft Geschäfte zu machen.
- Grußformel

Here is some help for you.

Telefonanlagen	telephone systems
anspruchsvoll	up-market
bedauern	to regret
Einbau	installation
seefest	seaworthy
Skonto	cash discount
jdn.'s Erwartungen entsprechen	to meet s.b.'s expectations
den Erfordernissen der europäischen Sicherheitsvorschriften entsprechen	to meet the requirements of the European safety regulations

Telcom

28 Wakefield Street
Sheffield 8VE17
Tel: 2662042
Fax: 2772042
E-Mail:
Telcom@britcom.co.uk

Your ref:
Our ref:
Date:

A Telephone Call

Switchboard:	Office Equipment Ltd, good morning. What can I do for you?
Debbie Morris:	Good morning. I'd like to speak to Mr Gibson from the purchasing department, please.
Switchboard:	Yes, hang on for a moment, please. I'll put you through.
Paul Gibson:	Paul Gibson speaking. How can I help you?
Debbie Morris:	Good morning, Mr Gibson. This is Debbie Morris from Telecommunications Ltd.
Paul Gibson:	Good morning, Ms Morris. I remember, we've done business before.
Debbie Morris:	Yes, you bought some fax machines. Mr Gibson, have you seen our latest advertisements with our special offer?
Paul Gibson:	No, I'm sorry, I haven't had the time yet.
Debbie Morris:	Well, then I'll try to give you a bit of information. We are offering our latest product, a *video-phone,* at an introductory price of 370 Euro for a period of 4 weeks.
Paul Gibson:	That's interesting for us, as we've just decided to expand our range of products. A *video-phone* fits into our collection. Could you please send us information on this product – or send us a sample, if possible?
Debbie Morris:	Look, I'm sorry, but time's getting rather short. It might be better to arrange a meeting at your company's head quarters. I'll show you the product and we'll discuss all details of terms and discounts. And if you're interested, you can fill in the order form at once and get the special offer price.
Paul Gibson:	Good idea! Would it be possible for you to come this week?
Debbie Morris:	Well, I'll just check my schedule. How about this Friday?
Paul Gibson:	That's fine. Shall we say at 11 o'clock?
Debbie Morris:	11 o'clock is OK by me. See you then, good-bye.
Paul Gibson:	Thanks for calling, good-bye.

Questions

a) What does the caller want?

b) Does the caller already know Mr Gibson?

c) Which product does the caller offer?

d) Why is Mr G. interested in this product?

e) Why does the caller suggest a meeting?

f) When will they meet?

Was sagen/schreiben Sie, wenn

a) Sie sich erinnern, mit jdm. schon Geschäfte gemacht zu haben?

b) Sie jdn. fragen, ob er Ihre aktuelle Werbeanzeige über ein Sonderangebot gesehen hat?

c) Sie ein aktuelles Produkt für einen Zeitraum von ... Wochen anbieten?

d) Sie beschlossen haben, Ihr Sortiment zu erweitern?

e) Sie jdn. bitten, Ihnen Informationen und ein Muster zuzuschicken?

f) Sie jdm. sagen wollen, dass die Zeit knapp wird?

g) Sie ein Treffen vorschlagen?

h) Sie jdn. fragen, ob es ihm möglich ist, in dieser Woche zu kommen?

i) Sie den Freitag (als Termin) vorschlagen?

j) Sie sich für den Anruf bedanken?

Language Practice

We have used the word: **'verb/action'** many times in the earlier units of this book. A verb/action is, of course, something you do! (*Handlung*). Now consider the following sentence:
   *Our company **has received** a number of offers.*

We must note two pieces of information from this sentence.

- The verb/action is 'to receive' and that action **happened in the past!**
- That verb/action has a consequence **now!**

What is that consequence?	– You can imagine: there are many offers lying on the Purchasing Manager's desk **(now).**
Why are they lying on the desk?	– Because other companies sent them **(past action).**

When these two points fit together, i.e.:
   *The verb/action happened in the past **and** the effect of that action is now,*

we must use the **present perfect tense.**

Here are some key words to help you remember to use this tense:
   since, for, recently, just, (not) yet …

It is very easy to form this tense: Simply follow the formula below!

> (the correct form of the helping verb) **to have + 3rd form of the verb/action**

Now let us look at some examples.

   *The prices **have changed.***

The verb/action is <u>to change</u> – and that action happened in the past. We do **not** know when; but that isn't important. The consequence of that change is **now.** If you order goods now, you must pay the new price.

   *Our stock of MasterBlaster soundcards **has run out.***

The verb/action is <u>to run out of something.</u> The consequence (or effect) is: There aren't any soundcards!

We can also use this tense in the **passive voice.** The points are still the same; but we must use an extra helping verb – ***the form is always 'been'.*** Note the following example!

   *Arrangements **have** already <u>**been**</u> made for your goods to be delivered.*

The formula for **present perfect passive** sentences is as follows:

> (correct form of) **to have + been + 3rd form of verb/action**

Language Practice

What do you say/write when ...?
Use the words in brackets to help you.

(1) Company X sent invoice no. 231 last Wednesday; and that invoice is lying on your desk. (receive)

We _____.

(2) You have been typing enquiry letters all day; and there are 10 letters lying on your desk. (write)

I _____.

(3) Your boss asked you to find out more information about a product; and you are waiting for answers to letters you wrote asking for further information. (request)

My boss _____.

(4) It is 12:00, you are in the canteen. You bought fish and chips; but now there is nothing left on your plate. (eat)

I _____.

(5) Your company planned to expand their range of products at the last meeting; everybody knows those plans now. (make arrangements)

Arrangements _____.

(6) Some weeks ago your company ordered goods and you are waiting for them to arrive. Your boss asks you: (arrive)

_____.

(7) Your colleague asked you to speak to Mr Gibson about your new fax machines. He now wants to know: (speak)

_____.

(8) You wanted to write some letters this morning but there were a lot of other things to do (not write).

I _____

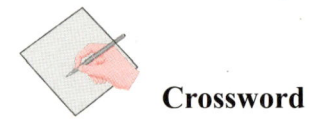

Crossword

Across

- 1 A: Preis angeben, nennen
- 1 I: jetzt
- 1 M: werben für, inserieren
- 3 C: Prospekt, Reklamezettel
- 3 T: in, innen
- 5 E: Dose
- 5 I: Kunde
- 6 S: rot
- 7 A: Antwort, Entgegnung
- 7 L: Muster
- 7 T: nein
- 9 J: Anlage (Kurzform)
- 9 O: Waren, Güter
- 11 A: Produkt
- 11 J: deshalb, so
- 12 L: Gebühr (Mz.)
- 14 N: Art, freundlich
- 15 E: Merkmal, Kennzeichen, vorkommen
- 16 M: zeigen, anzeigen
- 17 B: Handel
- 18 H: da, dort
- 20 A: weit, groß
- 20 G: Gesellschaft, Firma
- 22 O: völlig, total (Adv.)
- 23 A: Bitte, Wunsch, Ersuchen
- 23 J: Firma, fest
- 25 E: Bauernhof
- 25 J: zusätzlich
- 27 B: Träne
- 27 G: traurig
- 27 O: nah, nahe
- 29 B: (An-)Lieferung
- 29 N: Hitze
- 31 A: Arbeit, arbeiten
- 31 Q: Küste
- 33 D: Repräsentant, Vertreter
- 34 R: Werkzeug
- 36 A: nicht
- 36 E: Hund
- 36 K: Zigarette (Mz.)
- 38 L: gewähren
- 38 R: Dame

Down

- 1 E: genau, exakt (Adv.)
- 1 I: nicht
- 1 M: Zustimmung, Anerkennung
- 1 Q: roh
- 1 T: Verschiffung, Sendung, Transport
- 3 G: Hauptstadt von England
- 4 J: Geschäft, Branche
- 6 Q: empfehlen
- 9 D: Bestellung
- 9 F: einschließen, enthalten
- 11 B: Erhalt, Quittung
- 11 N: Verpackung
- 13 H: Aufmerksamkeit
- 13 K: bevorzugen
- 13 T: unwiderruflich
- 16 D: Sortiment
- 16 Q: Sammlung
- 17 F: Ohr
- 19 O: (Preis-)Angebot
- 20 B: interessiert
- 22 L: Händler
- 23 G: (Geschäfts-)Bedingungen
- 24 U: beträchtlich
- 25 E: für
- 27 H: veranlassen
- 27 Q: Artikel
- 28 N: Schiff
- 29 C: verdienen
- 31 A: bereit sein, willens sein
- 31 J: Kontakt, kontaktieren
- 32 E: entscheiden
- 32 M: Manager
- 33 G: Sortiment
- 33 I: liefern, die Lieferung, Versorgung
- 34 R: völlig, total
- 36 C: auch

Crossword

Useful phrases: Offers

Opening

Thank you for We refer to	your enquiry of … 20 ..	asking for information	on about	our products our range of products our services

| We were pleased | to | read
hear | that you are interested in | the products | ⚙ |
| | | | | our range of products | ★ |

| ⚙ | that we offer |
| ★ | presented at the trade fair in … |

Background to company or products

We are	a well-known	English German	manufacturer wholesaler	of	high-quality	products	with

world-wide business relations

We	want would like	to point out	that	we	only produce offer a range of	exclusive high-quality up-market	products

made of natural raw materials
that meet the requirements of the European safety regulations

Answer to customer's requests

| Please find enclosed | our | latest
current | catalogue
price list
brochure | of our range of products |
| | | | terms of business | |

together with our order form

| As requested | we will send | the samples | | under separate cover |
| | | a collection of our samples | you requested | |

Quotation

| We are pleased | to submit | the following quotation: |
| | | a quotation for the following items: |

Prices

The	prices	are quoted	FOB Bremen	and include packing.
Our			ex works	
			DDP Bremen	

Discounts

We	can	grant	a	retail	discount of ... %
	are willing to	let you have		trade	
	are prepared to	allow you		quantity	
				a first order	

on list price			
on the net price			
on orders	worth	at least .... €	
		.... € and/or more	

Delivery

Shipment	can	be	arranged	immediately	after	receipt	of	order
Delivery	will		made	within 2 weeks		confirmation		your order
	is usually							

| by | ship |
| | rail |

If you want	delivery	by	air freight	an	extra	charge will be made
			ship		additional	
	special delivery					

The goods are packed in seaworthy boxes

83

Payment

As we have not done business before	we request	payment	by

confirmed and irrevocable letter of credit

For first orders	payment should be effected	documents against payment
	our terms of payment are	

Closing

We	hope	that	our offer	meets	your expectations
	are sure		the quality of our products		with your approval
			our prices and terms	meet	your requirements

and that you	will	decide to	place	your order with us

Should you have any questions or require further information,	do not hesitate to

contact us

We	look forward to	doing business with you	in the near future

For special situations:

Regrets

We regret	that we cannot offer you	installation of our systems,

but we can recommend	our business partner T&H in Hamburg

Validity

This offer is	firm	for a period of ... weeks
	valid	

Special offer

May we draw your attention to	our special offer for tennis sportswear

Representative

As requested	our representative in Germany	will contact you	within this month

UNIT FOUR: **ORDERS**

Orders can be placed in two ways:

(1) The buyer replies to an offer, or
(2) The buyer contacts the seller directly (old customer).

When a company places an order, the buyer states that:

He or she is prepared to buy certain goods at the stated price and on the agreed terms.
Of course, the buyer will have to discuss the details with the seller. This can be done by post, telephone, fax or e-mail. If the buyer places an order by telephone, it is usual to confirm the order in writing.

Today, many firms use printed **order forms.** The buyer then fills in the form with the details the seller needs e.g. name, date, items, quantity, price etc.

The order which opens business relations between two firms is called an **initial order.** If the company needs some more goods, we call these **repeat orders.** If the company wants to order a small quantity of the product for testing, they will place a **trial order.**
Once an order has been placed it is binding!

Mark the following points as *true* or *false*.

		true	false
1.	Orders can be replies to offers.	☐	☐
2.	Orders should be confirmed in writing.	☐	☐
3.	Orders can **never** be placed by telephone.	☐	☐
4.	An initial order opens business relations between two firms.	☐	☐
5.	An initial order cancels all previous agreements.	☐	☐
6.	Buyers should draft their own order forms.	☐	☐
7.	You **must** use order forms when placing repeat orders.	☐	☐
8.	Trial orders are always for large quantities of the product.	☐	☐
9.	Trial orders are placed for testing purposes.	☐	☐
10.	Orders are binding.	☐	☐

Now summarize what you know about orders:

_____
_____
_____
_____
_____
_____
_____
_____
_____
_____

A Bill of Exchange is another common way of payment in foreign trade:

Germany		China
buyer / importer	←— contract of sale / payment by bill of exchange —→	seller / exporter
drawee / payer	←— fills in the draft and sends it to the drawee —— / —— signs the bill and accepts / a) to pay on demand (sight draft) / b) to pay on a fixed future date (time draft) —→	drawer / payee

The drawer can discount the bill of exchange to a bank, in this case the bank is the payee.

The Bike Shop

27 Brompton Road
London SW 11
Phone 01-370 2197
Fax   01-370 2198

Das Rad GmbH
Mr Patrick von Zahn
Breite Straße 12
28325 BREMEN
GERMANY

Your ref: PvZ/dl
Our ref: JC/dm
Date: 20 ..

Dear Mr von Zahn

Thank you for your offer of _____ 20. . and we are pleased to place the following order. (see *offer*)

    10 Mountain bikes *Hillclimber*   (blue)   at   220.00 € each
    10 Mountain bikes *Easybike*   (red)   at   210.00 € each

We understand that you are willing to grant us a retail discount of 15% and a further first order discount of 5%. We note that payment is to be effected by irrevocable and confirmed letter of credit.

As we need the bikes urgently, we would be grateful if you could arrange delivery as soon as possible.

Thank you for your trouble and we look forward to receiving the bicycles shortly.

Yours sincerely

John Clease
John Clease
Purchasing Manager

Questions

a) Who is the letter from?
b) Who is the letter to?
c) Why is the sender writing?
d) What is said about payment?
e) What is said about delivery of the bikes?
f) What is said about discounts?

The Bike Shop

27 Brompton Road

London SW 11
Phone 01-370 2197
Fax   01-370 2198

Das Rad GmbH
Mr von Zahn
Breite Straße 12
28325 BREMEN
GERMANY

Your ref: PvZ/dl
Our ref: JC/dm
Date: 20 ..

Fill in the gaps

Dear Mr von Zahn

Thank you for your offer of _____ 20 .. and we are pleased _____ the following _____.   (see *offer*)

      10 Mountain bikes *Hillclimber*   (blue)   at 220.00 € each
      10 Mountain bikes *Easybike*   (red)   at 210.00 € each

We_____ that you _____ to grant us a_____ of 15% and a further _____ of 5%.

We _____ that payment is to be _____ by irrevocable and confirmed letter of credit.

As we need the bikes _____, we would be grateful if you could arrange delivery _____.

Thank you for your _____ and we look forward to receiving the bicycles _____.

Yours sincerely

John Clease

John Clease
Purchasing Manager

(eine Bestellung) aufgeben	folgende, folgender
(einem Brief etc.) entnehmen	Händlerrabatt
(Zahlung) leisten	Mühe
bald	so schnell wie möglich
bereit sein	zur Kenntnis nehmen
dringend	Erstbestellungsrabatt

Was sagen/schreiben Sie, wenn

a) Sie erfreut sind, die folgende Bestellung aufzugeben?

b) Sie zur Kenntnis nehmen, dass die Bezahlung per L/C erfolgen soll?

c) Sie (dem Brief) entnehmen, dass die Firma bereit ist, Ihnen einen Händlerrabatt zu gewähren?

d) Sie sich für die Bemühungen der Firma bedanken?

e) Sie sich darauf freuen, bald die Fahrräder zu erhalten?

f) Sie (dem Brief) entnehmen, dass die Firma bereit ist, Ihnen einen weiteren Rabatt zu gewähren?

g) Sie dankbar dafür wären, wenn die Firma die Lieferung so schnell wie möglich veranlassen würde?

h) Sie sich freuen, die folgende Bestellung aufzugeben?

i) Sie die Waren dringend benötigen und daher für schnelle Lieferung dankbar wären?

Language Practice

When an action happened yesterday, last week, last month or even 5 minutes ago, we **must** use the **simple past tense.** We always use this tense to show that an action is finished.

Note: When we say **'finished'**, it means there is **no effect/consequence now!**
If there is an **effect/consequence now,** then we must use the *present perfect tense* (see page 78).

Using the **simple past tense** is easy when you remember that verbs/actions are either regular or irregular.

- The **regular verbs/actions** such as: receive, deliver, order, request, confirm etc. all have **'ed' endings**, i.e. receiv**ed**, deliver**ed**, order**ed**, request**ed**, confirm**ed** etc.

- You will have to **learn** the **irregular forms,** e.g. send [*sent - sent*], speak [*spoke - spoken*], write [*wrote - written*] etc., as **they do not follow any rules.**

Exercises

*Put the verbs and phrases in brackets into the correct form of the **simple past tense.***

(1) When we _____ *(to receive)* the goods, we _____ *(to find out)* that they _____ *(to be)* badly damaged.

(2) Unfortunately, you _____ *(not send)* the quantities we _____ *(to specify).*

(3) I _____ *(to inform)* the manager of the delivery dates last Wednesday.

(4) We are pleased to inform you that the goods _____ *(to be shipped)* last Monday on board 'SS-Dedlos', which _____ *(to leave)* the port of Hamburg the same evening.

(5) Your secretary _____ *(to tell)* me that you _____ *(not take)* sugar or milk in your coffee.

(6) _____ you _____ *(to place)* the order with 'FreeTel'?

Yes, I _____ *(to place)* the order by telephone, and _____ *(to confirm)* the order in writing.

Exercises

Put the verbs and phrases in brackets into the correct form. Remember, this time you must ask yourself: Is the action finished? Does the action have an effect/consequence now?
*Use the **simple past** tense or **present perfect** tense in your answers.*

(1) The Customs Inspector *(to inspect)* the goods when they *(to arrive)* at the port.

_____

(2) 'When *(you receive)* my initial order?'

_____

(3) 'My boss is very busy, he *(to write)* twenty letters of enquiry this morning'.

_____

(4) The manager isn't in at the moment. He *(to go)* to a meeting in London.

_____

(5) The manager isn't in at the moment; he *(to go)* to London at 8:00 this morning.

_____

(6) 'We are sorry for the delay in delivery, but we *(to have)* problems with our suppliers'.

_____

(7) 'I *(not have)* a holiday since I *(to start)* working here'.

_____

(8) 'We *(to receive)* your order and will give it our prompt attention.

_____

(9) 'I'm sorry, Mr Gibson *(to be out)* all morning. He *(to leave)* at 8:30 this morning.

_____

(10) As we *(not do)* business before, we *(to request)* payment by irrevocable and confirmed letter of credit.

_____

Draft a letter.

Sie sind Inge Langer von der Firma *Das Rad* und schreiben eine Bestellung an die Firma *Lung Mingh Ltd.*

- Beziehen Sie sich auf das Angebot vom … (siehe *offer*).

- Da die Tests des Musterdynamos zufriedenstellend waren, sind Sie erfreut die folgende Bestellung aufzugeben:

- 1.000 Dynamos FX 37 à 10,00 €

- Sie erwarten, dass die Dynamos von derselben Qualität wie die Muster sind.

- Sie nehmen zur Kenntnis, dass *Lung Mingh* bereit ist, Ihnen einen Händlerrabatt von 5% zu gewähren.

- Die Zahlung erfolgt *Dokumente gegen Bezahlung*.

- Sie entnehmen den Geschäftsbedingungen, dass die Lieferung innerhalb von 10 Tagen nach Erhalt der Bestellung erfolgen kann.

- Sie erwarten die Waren daher bis spätestens … (Datum).

- Sie freuen sich, die Dynamos zum fälligen Termin zu erhalten.

- Grußformel

Here is some help for you.

erwarten	to expect

zufriedenstellend	satisfactory

innerhalb von 10 Tagen	within 10 days

nach Erhalt	after receipt

Das Rad GmbH
Breite Straße 12
28325 Bremen
Tel: +49 421 361-18263
Fax: +49 421 361-18264

Ihr Zeichen:　　　　　Unser Zeichen:　　　　　Bremen,

Crossword

1
2
3
4
5
6
7
8
9

Translate the following sentences and fill in the above crossword.

(1) Wir hoffen, dass Sie mit der **Qualität** unserer Ware zufrieden sind.

_____

(2) Die Zahlung soll per **Dokumente** gegen Kasse erfolgen.

_____

(3) Wir **entnehmen** Ihrem Brief, dass die Ware per Eilzustellung geliefert wird.

_____

(4) Wir **erwarten**, dass die Ware von der gleichen Qualität wie die Muster ist.

_____

(5) Wir sind erfreut, dass Sie uns einen Rabatt von 5% **gewähren**.

_____

(6) Die Lieferung erfolgt 10 Tage nach **Erhalt** der Bestellung (Auftragseingang).

_____

(7) Wir können **innerhalb** von 10 Tagen liefern.

_____

(8) Unsere Tests waren **zufriedenstellend.**

_____

(9) Wir **entnehmen** Ihrem Brief, dass die Zahlung per *Dokumente gegen Kasse* erfolgen soll.

_____

Crossword

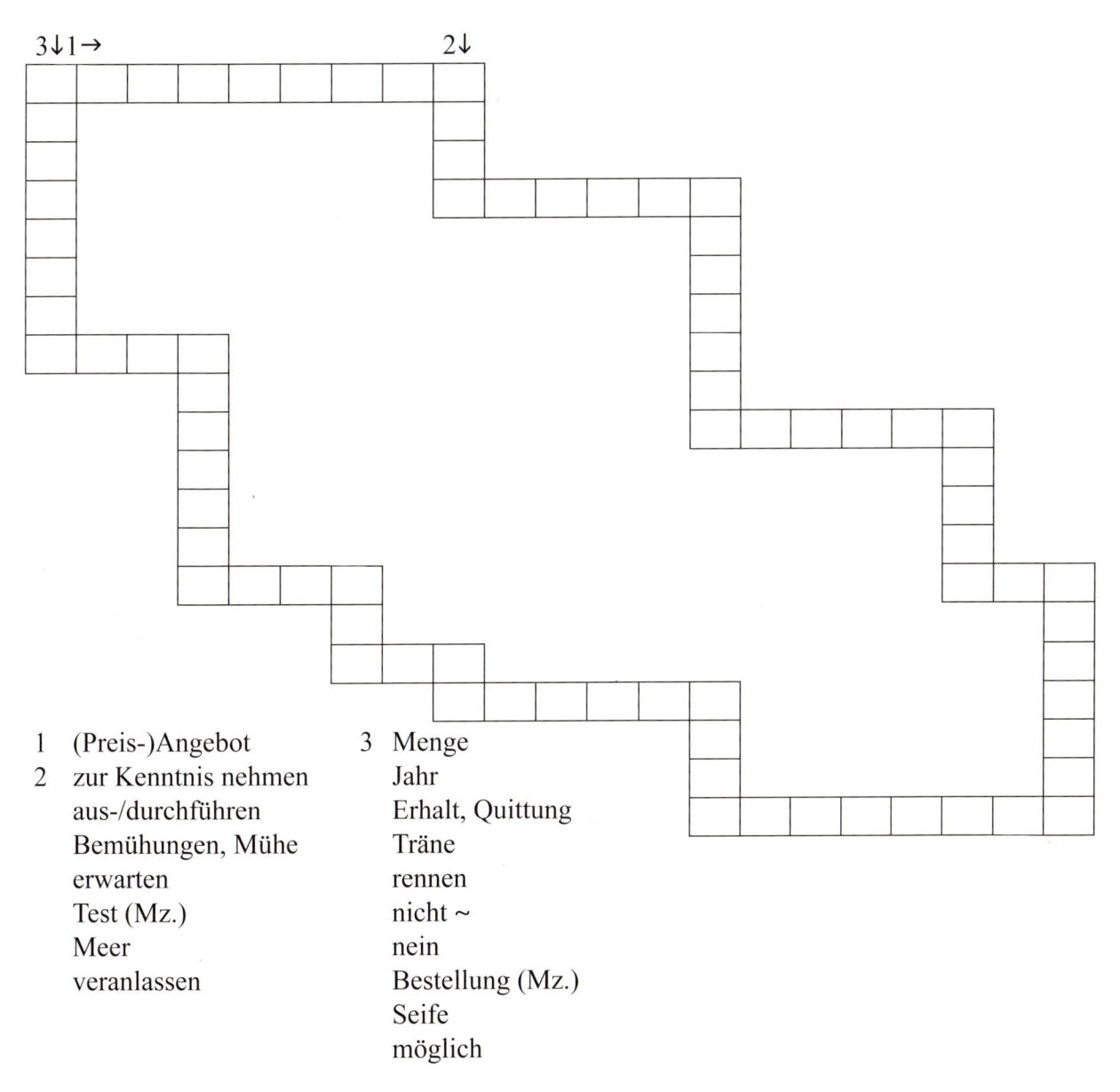

3↓ 1→   2↓

1. (Preis-)Angebot
2. zur Kenntnis nehmen
   aus-/durchführen
   Bemühungen, Mühe
   erwarten
   Test (Mz.)
   Meer
   veranlassen
3. Menge
   Jahr
   Erhalt, Quittung
   Träne
   rennen
   nicht ~
   nein
   Bestellung (Mz.)
   Seife
   möglich

Now make your own sentences using as many words as possible from the crossword above.

_____
_____
_____
_____
_____
_____
_____

Draft a letter.

Sie sind Sharon Dearns, Mitarbeiterin der Firma *Sportmexx*. Sie haben das Angebot der Firma *Sport + Spaß* bearbeitet und schreiben eine Bestellung.

- Bedanken Sie sich für den Katalog und die Preisliste.
- Sie haben einige Muster der Sportbekleidung untersucht und sind mit der Qualität sehr zufrieden.
- Daher möchten Sie die unten aufgeführten Waren bestellen. Das Auftragsformular ist beigefügt.
- Die von *Sport + Spaß* in den Geschäftsbedingungen angegebenen Preise gelten ab Werk und gelten einschließlich Verpackung.
- Sie entnehmen (dem Angebot), dass *Sport+Spaß* bereit ist, Ihnen einen Erstauftragsrabatt von 3 % zukommen zu lassen.
- Zahlung erfolgt wie festgelegt mit bestätigtem unwiderruflichen Akkreditiv.
- Sie bitten darum, dass *Sport+Spaß* diesen Auftrag nur annimmt, wenn *Sport + Spaß* innerhalb von zwei Wochen nach Auftragseingang liefern kann, da Sie die Waren zum Beginn der Sommersaison benötigen.
- Sie hoffen, dass *Sport + Spaß* Ihrem Auftrag sofortige Aufmerksamkeit zukommen lassen wird und dass dies der Anfang einer langen und erfreulichen Geschäftsbeziehung sein wird.
- Grußformel

- Bestellen Sie auf dem beigefügten Auftragsformular von Sport + Spaß:

    150 Stück, T-Shirts, Artikel-Nr. 93331 à   20,10 €
     75 Stück, Fußballtrikots, Artikel-Nr. 2482 à   22,00 €
    120 Stück, Fußballhosen, Artikel-Nr. 2472 à   16,20 €
     50 Stück, Tennishemden, Artikel-Nr. 1397 à   15,40 €

Here is some help for you.

to examine	untersuchen
as stipulated	wie festgelegt
to accept	annehmen
pleasant business relationship	erfreuliche Geschäftsbeziehung
prompt attention	sofortige Aufmerksamkeit

Sportmexx
43 Station Road
Fakenham
Norfolk NR 12 7 GH
Tel: 876620   Fax: 886620

Your ref:
Our ref:
Date:

Sport + Spaß

Walliser Straße 125
28325 Bremen
Tel: 0421 361-2728 – Fax: 0421 361-2245

ORDER FORM				No.	328
Customer: **Customer's No.:**		**Address:**			
Article No	Quantity	Description	List Price/Item	Discount	Total

Signature: _____   Date: _____

Translate the following sentences and fill in the crossword.

1. Wir sind mit der Qualität Ihrer **Sportbekleidung** sehr zufrieden.
   _____

2. Wir entnehmen Ihrem Angebot, dass die Preise **ab Werk** sind.
   _____

3. Diese Bestellung ist nur **gültig,** wenn Sie innerhalb von zwei Wochen liefern können.
   _____

4. Wir möchten **daher** die folgende Bestellung aufgeben.
   _____

5. Wir hoffen, dass Sie diesem Auftrag **sofortige** Aufmerksamkeit zukommen lassen werden.
   _____

98

Crossword

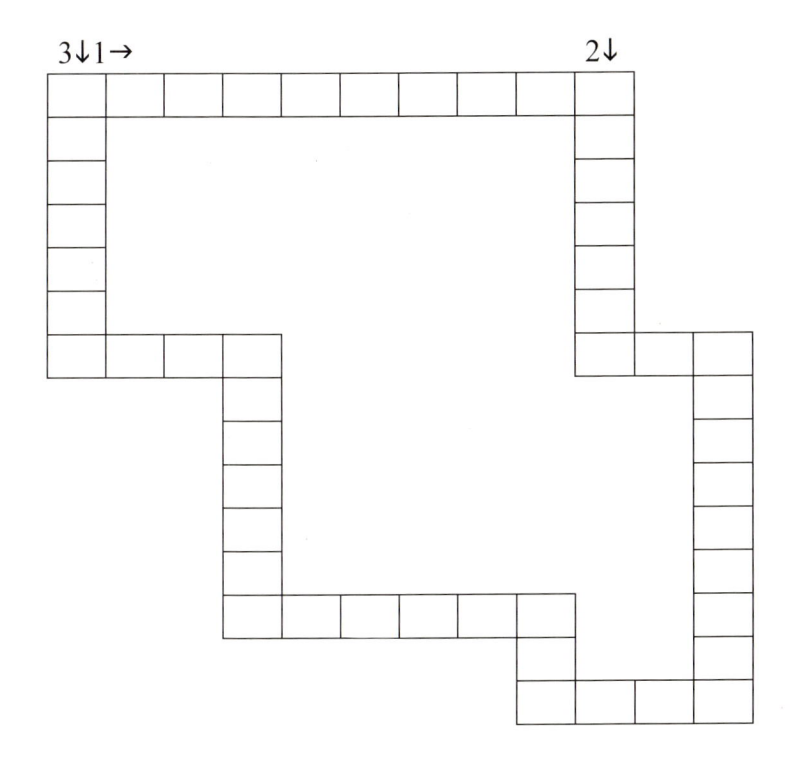

3↓ 1→   2↓

1 Begleichung, Bezahlung
2 Mühe
   Ende, enden
   Rabatt (Mz.)
3 in Kürze
   Jahr
   erhalten
   erwarten
   der, die, das
   Anlage (Mz., Kurzform)

Fill in suitable words from the crossword above.

1. We request _____ by irrevocable letter of credit.

2. We hope to hear from you _____ .

3. We _____ delivery within 10 days.

4. *CompaTec* will grant a _____ of 3 %.

5. Thank you for your _____ .

6. *Vobas Computers* will _____ the goods next week.

99

Draft a letter.

Sie sind die Mitarbeiterin Eva Müller von der Firma *Vobas Computers* und schreiben eine Bestellung an die Firma *CompaTec*.

- Bedanken Sie sich für das Angebot vom … (siehe *offer*).
- Sie sind erfreut, eine Bestellung für die unten aufgeführten Waren aufzugeben.
- In der Anlage übersenden Sie Ihr Auftragsformular.
- Sie nehmen zur Kenntnis, dass alle Preise DDP Bremen sind.
- Da Sie die Waren dringend benötigen, bitten Sie um Lieferung per Luftfracht.
- Wie gewünscht wird die Bezahlung *Bezahlung gegen Dokumente* erfolgen.
- Sie nehmen zur Kenntnis, dass *CompaTec* bereit ist, Ihnen einen Erstbestellungsrabatt von 3 % und einen weiteren Mengenrabatt von 5 % zu gewähren.
- Sie freuen sich darauf, die Waren in Kürze zu erhalten.
- Grußformel

- Bestellen Sie auf dem beigefügten Auftragsformular von *Vobas Computers*:

- 1.000 Soundkarten à   38,50 € pro Stück
- 1.500 Lautsprecher à   30,00 € pro Paar

VOBAS COMPUTERS

Pappelstraße 54
28199 Bremen
Tel: +49 421 2592923

ORDER No _____						
Article No.	Quantity	Description	List Price/Item	Discount	Total

Date/Signature: _____

VOBAS COMPUTERS

Pappelstraße 54
28199 Bremen
Tel: +49 421 2592

Ihre Zeichen   Unsere Zeichen   Bremen,

Draft a letter.

Sie heißen Inge Langer und haben das Angebot der Firma *Telcom* bearbeitet. Schreiben Sie eine Bestellung.

- Beziehen Sie sich auf den Besuch des Vertreters Herrn Bush in der vergangenen Woche.
- Teilen Sie mit, dass Herr Bush Ihnen die notwendigen Informationen über das Sortiment an hochwertigen Telefonsystemen gegeben hat.
- Er hat Ihnen empfohlen, zwei unterschiedliche Systeme einzubauen.
- Weisen Sie auf Ihr beigefügtes Auftragsformular hin.
- Wie mit Herrn Bush besprochen, freuen Sie sich zu bemerken, dass *Telcom* bereit ist, Ihnen einen speziellen Mengenrabatt von 5 % für Aufträge über 250 Stück zu gewähren.
- Sie nehmen zur Kenntnis, dass die angegebenen Preise ab Werk einschließlich Verpackung in seefesten Kisten gelten.
- Sie werden die Bezahlung durchführen, indem Sie ein unwiderrufliches bestätigtes Akkreditiv zugunsten von *Telcom* bei Ihrer Bank eröffnen.
- Sie bitten darum, dass *Telcom* Sie benachrichtigt, sobald die Waren versandt worden sind. Dann können Sie den sofortigen Einbau der Geräte mit *Technik & Hilfe* vereinbaren.
- Sie erwarten, innerhalb der nächsten Wochen die Versandanzeige zu erhalten.
- Grußformel

- Bestellen Sie auf dem beigefügten Bestellformular Ihrer Firma:

125 Geräte Telcom System 300 AKH	375,00 €
245 Geräte Telcom System 217 QHP	156,00 €

Here you can find all the help you need.

(to) expect		gave
	discussed	
(to) refer		(to) advise
	have been dispatched	
advised		(to) understand
	are pleased	
will effect		(to) include
	are prepared	
can arrange		(to) find
	are	

Das Rad GmbH
Breite Straße 12
28325 Bremen
Tel: +49 421 361-18263
Fax: +49 421 361-18264

Ihr Zeichen: Unser Zeichen: Bremen,

Das Rad GmbH   Breite Straße 12 28325 Bremen
Tel: +49 421 361-18263 Fax: 361-18264

ORDER No. 384

Article No.	Quantity	Description	List Price/Item	Discount	Total

Signature: _____   Date: _____

Match the German sentences with the English expressions.

1) We understand that prices are ex works.

2) Please find enclosed our order form.

3) We will effect payment by letter of credit.

4) As discussed you will grant us a discount of 5%.

a) Wir zahlen per Akkreditiv.

b) Wie besprochen gewähren Sie uns einen Rabatt von 5%.

c) Wir entnehmen (Ihrem Schreiben), dass die Preise ab Werk sind.

d) In der Anlage übersenden wir unser Bestellformular.

Fill in the table with suitable verbs and nouns.

Nouns	Verbs	Nouns	Verbs
need			to arrange
request			to receive
understanding			to expect
confirmation			to satisfy
demand			to pay

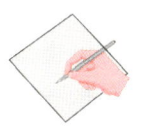

Now fill in the gaps with suitable words from the list above.

1. As there is a great _____ for bicycles especially in the summer months we _____ the dynamos as soon as possible.

2. We will deliver the goods within 10 days of _____ of your order.

3. _____ have already been made for your goods to be delivered.

4. As _____ the goods will be delivered by air freight.

5. We _____ from your letter that you are willing to grant us a retail discount of 5%.

6. We are sure that the quality of our product meets your _____.

7. _____ has to be effected by banker's draft.

8. We request payment by _____ irrevocable letter of credit.

9. Our products are guaranteed to give complete _____.

10. *Popeye PLC* _____ payment within 10 days of delivery.

A Telephone Call

Switchboard:	Telecommunications Ltd., good morning, can I help you?
Paul Gibson:	Good morning, Paul Gibson here, can I speak to Ms Morris in the Sales Department, please.
Switchboard:	Certainly, hold the line please, I'll put you through. Sorry, what did you say your name was?
Paul Gibson:	Paul Gibson.
Switchboard:	Thank you.
Debbie Morris:	Good morning, can I help you?
Paul Gibson:	Yes, I received your offer for telephone answering machines and suitable cassettes yesterday and would like to place an order with you.
Debbie Morris:	Fine, if you give me the details, I'll just make some notes.
Paul Gibson:	Right, I'd like 200 answering machines AM 300 and 200 cassettes CA300. Can I just confirm the price? In your offer you wrote the unit price was 30.00 € for the answering machines and 3.00 € for the cassettes. Was that a firm offer?
Debbie Morris:	Yes, that's right, but those prices will change in 6 months.
Paul Gibson:	Now, the answering machines have to be delivered together with the cassettes.
Debbie Morris:	That's no problem. Delivery will be made by next week at the latest. – Can I ask you to settle the invoice by Banker's Draft?
Paul Gibson:	Sure, that's no problem at all.
Debbie Morris:	Fine, can I ask you to confirm this order in writing?
Paul Gibson:	I'll send the written order to you by post this afternoon and I look forward to receiving the goods by next week.
Debbie Morris:	Thank you very much for your call, Mr Gibson.
Paul Gibson:	No trouble at all, good bye.
Debbie Morris:	Good bye.

Draft a short message.

- Sie beziehen sich auf das Telefonat von heute morgen und bestätigen die Bestellung der auf dem Auftragsformular aufgeführten Artikel.
- Grußformel

Dear _____

Fill in the order form.

Office Equipment
25 Bolton Gardens
London SW 1
Tel: 044 1278 77329
Fax: 044 1278 78329

Quantity	Item description	Cat.No.	Unit Price

Date, Signature _____

Was sagen/schreiben Sie, wenn

a) Sie fragen, ob Sie mit Herrn Murray von der Verkaufsabteilung sprechen können?
Can I
- [ ] speak Mr Murray in the Sales Department, please.
- [ ] speak to Mr Murray in the Sales Department, please.
- [ ] to speak Mr Murray in the Sales Department, please.

b) Sie nochmals nach dem Namen des Anrufers fragen?
Sorry, what
- [ ] did your name?
- [ ] did you say ?
- [ ] did you say your name was?

c) Sie sich ein paar Notizen machen?
I'll just
- [ ] note something.
- [ ] make some notes.
- [ ] notice something.

d) Sie mitteilen, dass sich die Preise in 3 Monaten ändern?
The prices
- [ ] change in 3 months.
- [ ] are changing in 3 months.
- [ ] will change in 3 months.

e) Sie darauf hinweisen, dass die Anrufbeantworter mit den Kassetten geliefert werden müssen?
The answering machines
- [ ] have to deliver together with the cassettes.
- [ ] have been delivered together with the cassettes.
- [ ] have to be delivered together with the cassettes.

f) Sie versichern, dass es keine Probleme (mit der Bitte Ihres Gesprächspartners) gibt?
That's
- [ ] not the problem.
- [ ] null problemo.
- [ ] no problem.

Crossword

Across

1 A: (Be)Zahlung
1 I: Erstauftrag
2 N: von
3 A: und
3 E: pro, je
3 I: Brief
4 O: bestätigen
5 A: erwarten
5 H: für
5 T: mich
6 K: Wunsch, Bitte
7 D: roh
8 I: zur Kenntnis nehmen, Notiz
8 O: gewähren
9 E: in
9 K: auf
10 O: frei
11 A: Absprache, Vereinbarung
11 M: nach, hinter
12 S: sie
13 K: Angebot
14 C: Recht, richtig
15 A: dann
15 G: Straße (Mz.)
15 M: Rabatt
7 A: Ei
17 E: du
17 I: zufriedenstellend
19 C: Probeauftrag
19 O: laut

Down

1 A: (Bestellung) aufgeben, Platz
1 E: Erwartung
1 G: Trimester
1 I: folgende, folgender
1 L: Begleichung, Bezahlung
1 O: von
1 Q: runter, unten
2 N: oder
2 T: Formular
3 C: Abteilung (Abkürzung)
4 U: mittel
6 Q: Händler
8 O: Geschenk
9 A: garantieren
9 C: Luftfracht
10 P: Referenz (Abkürzung)
11 K: auch
11 T: bald
14 G: Mühe
15 O: klein
17 I: Schau
17 M: sicher
17 Q: wahr

Useful phrases: Orders

Opening

Thank you for	your	offer of .... 20 .. catalogue and price list	and	we are pleased	to place the following order
We refer to	your	quotation of ..... 20 .. offer			
		representative's visit	at our	head office	last week

Background to your order

| Mr Bush Your representative | gave us | all the necessary | information | on your range of | up-market |

telephone systems

| We have | examined | some | samples of your | sportswear | and | we are satisfied with the quality |

| As | our tests | of the | sample dynamos | were | satisfactory | we are pleased | to place |

the following order

Order

We would like	to place	the following	order
	to order		goods
		the goods	listed below

| Please find enclosed | your | order form |
| | our | |

Prices

| Prices | as | stated | in your terms | are | ex works | and include | packing | in seaworthy boxes. |

110

Discounts

We	are	pleased	to note	that you are	prepared	to	allow	us	a special
		understand			willing		grant		
							let us have		

quantity first order retail	discount	of ...%	for an order	of	250	units		
			and	a	further	quantity first order retail	discount	of ...%
				an	additional			

Payment

We	will	effect	payment		by	irrevocable and confirmed letter of credit
	note	that		has to be effected		documents against payment
Payment		will be made				banker's draft

Additional information/requests

Please	advise us	as soon as	the goods	have been	dispatched

This order	is only valid if you	can	deliver	within	two weeks	after	receipt	of this	order

As	we	need	the	goods	urgently	we	request
		require		bicycles	for the beginning of this summer season		

delivery	by	air freight
		as soon as possible

We	expect	to receive	the goods	in the next weeks
			your advice of dispatch	shortly

Closing

We	hope	that	you	will	give	this	order	your	prompt and careful attention
	look forward to				receiving	the	goods	shortly	
								by the due date	

UNIT FIVE: ACKNOWLEDGEMENTS AND DISPATCH NOTES

These are short written messages in reply to orders. When a company receives an order, it is usual for them to answer quickly; this answer is called an **acknowledgement.** It is often the written confirmation of a deal.

Usually, an acknowledgement will thank the customer and point out when the goods will be delivered. If the company can deliver the goods immediately, they will probably not send an acknowledgement, but send a **dispatch note**/an **advice of dispatch** which tells the buyer when he or she can expect the goods. It will often confirm the type and number of goods ordered and should correspond with the goods enclosed in the shipment.

Mark the following points as *true* or *false*.

		true	false
1.	Today no companies send letters of acknowledgement.	☐	☐
2	Acknowledgements are detailed explanations of dates of delivery.	☐	☐
3.	Acknowledgements are confirmations of deals.	☐	☐
4.	Dispatch notes tell the buyer what is in the shipment.	☐	☐
5.	Dispatch notes are usually sent when the goods are dispatched immediately.	☐	☐

Now summarize what you know about acknowledgements and dispatch notes.

_____
_____
_____
_____
_____
_____
_____
_____

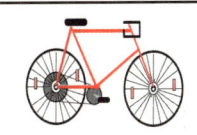

Mr J. Clease
The Bike Shop
27 Brompton Road
LONDON SW 11
ENGLAND

Das Rad GmbH
Breite Straße 12
28325 Bremen
Tel: +49 421 361-18263
Fax: +49 421 361-18264
Your ref: JC/dm
Our ref: PvZ/dl
Date:

Dear Mr Clease

Order Acknowledgement

Thank you for your order of … 20 . . (see *order*) for bicycles to the total value of 3,440.00 € after the agreed discount of 20 %.

We confirm delivery of the bicycles within 10 days of this acknowledgement of your order. Our Dispatch Department has been instructed accordingly.

We note that settlement will be effected by irrevocable and confirmed letter of credit.

We thank you for placing your order with us.

You can be sure that the quality of our bicycles will meet with your approval.

Yours sincerely
Das Rad GmbH

Patrick von Zahn

Patrick von Zahn
Sales Manager

Questions

a) What does this letter refer to?
b) What is the purpose of this letter?
c) How will settlement be effected?
d) When will delivery be arranged?
e) What is the total value of this order?
f) What has the Dispatch Department been instructed to do?

Crossword

```
1
2
3
4
5
6
7
8
9
10
```

Translate the following sentences and fill in the above crossword

1. Sie können **sicher** sein, dass wir pünktlich liefern. *(on time)*

   _____

2. Die **Lieferung** erfolgt innerhalb von 10 Tagen.

   _____

3. Der **Gesamt**preis beträgt 100,00 €.

   _____

4. Danke für Ihren **Brief** vom … 20 ..

   _____

5. Wir verkaufen qualitativ hochwertige **Fahrräder.**

   _____

6. Die Zahlung **erfolgt** durch Akkreditiv.

   _____

7. Wir **bestätigen** die Lieferung bis zum 15. 2. 20 ..

   _____

8. Wir freuen uns, die folgende **Bestellung** aufzugeben.

   _____

9. Wir liefern innerhalb von 2 Wochen nach Auftrags**bestätigung.**

   _____

10. Wir **nehmen zur Kenntnis,** dass Sie Eilzustellung wünschen.

    _____

Lung Mingh Ltd 23 Xingh Mu Beijing Republic of China Telephone: 008610 543764 Fax: 008610 543765

Your ref: IL/dl
Our ref: ZJ/sd
Date:

Dear Ms Langer

Order _acknowledgement_

Thank you _for_ your order _dated_ 20 ..

We _were_ pleased to _read_ that you were _satisfied_ with the _quality_ of our dynamo FX 37.

This letter is to _confirm_ that our prices and _discounts_ are as follows:

1,000 Dynamos FX 37,   list price: 10.00 €   net value: 10,000.00 €

We must _draw_ your attention _to_ the fact that a _trade_ discount will only _be granted_ on orders worth _at least_ 12,500.00 €.

As the items are _in stock_, we are able to _arrange_ immediate delivery. You can _expect_ the goods by (date)_____ at the latest.

The goods _will be_ packed in _wooden_ boxes with _metal_ bands.

Our _freight_ forwarder has been _instructed_ accordingly.

As _stated_ in our offer, our terms of _payment_ are documents _against_ payment.

We feel _sure_ that the goods will meet your _expectations_.

Yours sincerely

Zhang Jin

Zhang Jin
Sales Manager

Choose the right words from the box and fill in the gaps:

acknowledgement - against - arrange - at least - be granted - confirm - dated - discounts - draw - expect - expectations - for freight - in stock - instructed - metal - payment - quality - read - satisfied - stated - sure - trade - to - were - will be - wooden

Was sagen/schreiben Sie, wenn

a) Sie die sofortige Lieferung veranlassen können?

b) die Waren in hölzernen Kisten mit Metallbändern verpackt sein werden?

c) Ihr Spediteur dementsprechend angewiesen worden ist?

d) Sie sicher sind, dass die Waren den Erwartungen (des Kunden) entsprechen werden?

e) es Sie gefreut hat zu lesen, dass (der Kunde) mit der Qualität Ihrer Produkte zufrieden war?

f) Sie mit diesem Brief bestätigen, dass folgende Preise und Rabatte gelten?

g) Sie sich für den Auftrag vom (*siehe Bestellung*) bedanken?

h) Sie die Aufmerksamkeit (des Kunden) auf die Tatsache lenken müssen, dass ein Händlerrabatt nur für Aufträge im Wert von mindestens … € gewährt wird?

i) die Waren auf Lager sind?

j) wie im Angebot angegeben, die Zahlungsbedingungen … sind?

Crossword

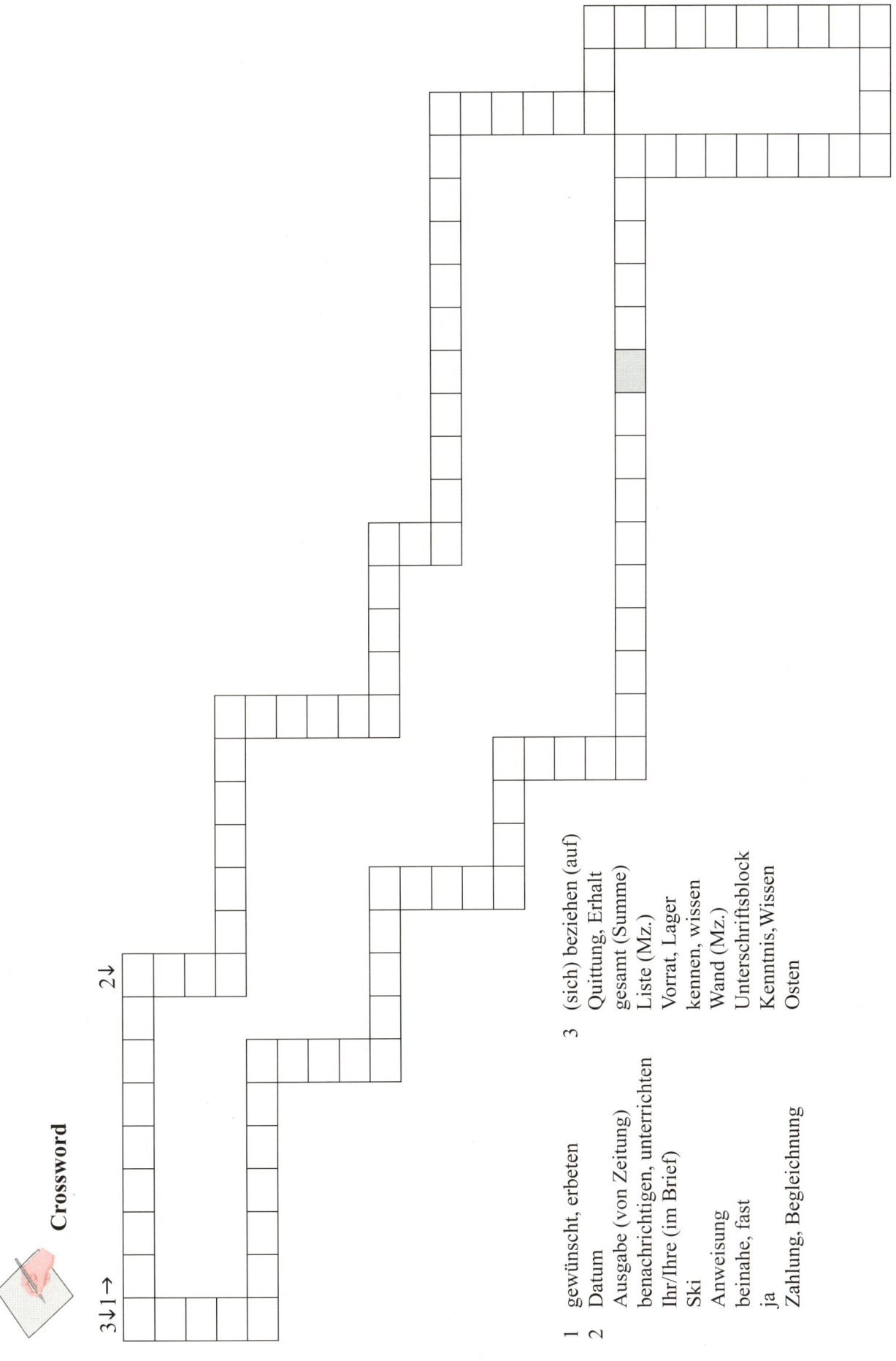

3↓ 1→

2↓

1 gewünscht, erbeten
2 Datum
   Ausgabe (von Zeitung)
   benachrichtigen, unterrichten
   Ihr/Ihre (im Brief)
   Ski
   Anweisung
   beinahe, fast
   ja
   Zahlung, Begleichung
3 (sich) beziehen (auf)
   Quittung, Erhalt
   gesamt (Summe)
   Liste (Mz.)
   Vorrat, Lager
   kennen, wissen
   Wand (Mz.)
   Unterschriftsblock
   Kenntnis, Wissen
   Osten

Draft a letter.

Sie heißen Gabriela Zastrow und arbeiten bei der Firma *Sport + Spaß* in Bremen. Sie beantworten den Auftrag der Firma *Sportmexx,* dem Sie die notwendigen Informationen entnehmen.

- Sie bedanken sich für den Auftrag vom ... (siehe *order*) für die unten aufgelisteten Artikel (Liste einfügen).
- Sie haben sich gefreut zu hören, dass *Sportmexx* von der Qualität Ihrer Produkte beeindruckt war.
- Der obige Auftrag von *Sportmexx* ist (zur Bearbeitung) weitergeleitet worden und Sie werden Ihr Bestes tun, um den Erwartungen von *Sportmexx* zu entsprechen.
- Da Sie ab Lager liefern können, können Sie *Sportmexx* zusichern, dass die Lieferung innerhalb zwei Wochen erfolgen wird.
- Die Waren werden in rückgabepflichtige Container verpackt.
- Sobald Sie die Bestätigung des Akkreditivs von Ihrer Bank erhalten haben, werden Sie die Waren versenden.
- Sie freuen sich darauf, von der sicheren Ankunft der Waren zu hören und bald weitere Aufträge von *Sportmexx* zu erhalten.
- Grußformel

Here is some help for you.

unten aufgelistet	listed below
beeindruckt sein	to be impressed
Ihr Auftrag ist (zur Bearbeitung) weitergeleitet worden	your order has been put in hand
sein Bestes tun	to do one's best
jdm. (etwas) versichern, zusichern	to assure
obig	above
ab Lager liefern	to supply/to deliver from stock
verpacken	to pack
rückgabepflichtig	returnable
Bestätigung	confirmation
versenden	to dispatch
sichere Ankunft	safe arrival

Sport + Spaß

Walliser Str. 125
28325 Bremen

Tel: 0421 361-2728
Fax: 0421 361-2245

Ihre Zeichen			Unsere Zeichen			Bremen,_____

Draft a letter by putting the phrases from the chart into the correct order.

Sie sind Alec Simon, Mitarbeiter der *Firma CompaTec,* und bearbeiten den Auftrag von *Vobas.*

- Sie freuen sich, *Vobas* zu informieren, dass die Waren, die *Vobas* am ... (siehe *order*) bestellt haben, jetzt versandbereit sind.
- Die Waren werden per Flugzeug als Eilfracht mit dem Lufthansa Flug Nr. 327 verschickt, der von London Heathrow um 14:30 Uhr am ..... *(Datum)* abfliegt. Die Waren sind in stabilen Kisten verpackt.
- In der Anlage übersenden Sie *Vobas* Ihre Rechnung Nr. 121 über den Gesamtpreis von 77.650,00 € einschließlich der Extragebühr für Eilluftfracht.
- Sie haben Ihre Korrespondenzbank, *Deutsche Bank AG* in Bremen, angewiesen, die Dokumente (Luftfrachtbrief, Packliste, Versicherungsschein) gegen Zahlung dieser Rechnung freizugeben.
- Sie vertrauen darauf, dass die Lieferung pünktlich und in gutem Zustand ankommen wird.
- Grußformel
- Anlagen

air waybill	packing list
insurance certificate	against payment
enc	*Alec Simon*
which leaves London Heathrow	at 14:30 on ... (date)
Yours sincerely	Dear Ms Müller
in sturdy cases	please find enclosed
including extra charge	for fast air freight.
the goods	have been packed
by air as fast freight	on Lufthansa Flight No 327
we have instructed	our correspondent bank
the consignment will arrive	punctually
and in good condition	that the goods ordered on ... *(see order)*
are now ready for dispatch.	the goods will be sent
we are pleased	to inform you
Deutsche Bank AG in Bremen	to release the documents
of this invoice	we trust
invoice no 121	advice of dispatch
our invoice no 121	for the total price of 77,650.00 €

CompaTec

35 Moseley Street
London SW 1
Tel.: 01-4674358
Fax: 01-4684359
E-mail: Compatec@britcom.co.uk

Your ref:
Our ref:
Date:

Answer the following questions about *CompaTec's* letter to *Vobas*.

1. Why does *CompaTec* write this letter to *Vobas*?
   _____

2. Will the goods be sent by normal air freight?
   _____

3. When does Flight No 327 leave Heathrow?
   _____

4. What is enclosed with this letter?
   _____

5. Which documents will be released to *Vobas* against payment of the invoice?
   _____

Find ten hidden words in this wordsquare and fill them in the gaps.

c	i	r	r	o	d	a	b	l	e	t	r	i	s	t	e	r	l	l	y	p
o	n	c	o	r	r	e	s	p	o	n	d	e	n	t	i	b	l	a	e	a
r	c	o	a	e	a	f	a	c	k	n	e	w	a	e	m	e	n	t	o	c
e	i	n	c	l	u	d	i	n	g	a	c	c	a	b	a	w	e	k	a	t
n	n	d	d	e	t	p	v	c	e	r	t	i	f	i	c	a	t	e	b	u
d	d	i	e	a	k	e	r	x	b	a	s	t	u	r	d	y	d	u	c	e
i	i	t	u	s	e	x	w	h	a	c	e	v	i	f	o	b	l	a	v	r
o	n	i	p	e	r	t	i	r	t	r	u	s	t	s	a	i	c	r	e	a
n	g	o	h	d	b	r	c	o	m	m	p	u	t	e	r	l	a	b	e	b
e	u	n	e	t	y	a	r	p	u	n	c	t	u	a	l	l	y	e	r	l
x	p	e	r	s	e	i	l	e	t	e	r	o	b	c	r	d	i	g	w	e

- After payment of the invoice the documents will be _____ .
- The sender _____ that the consignment will arrive _____ and in good _____ .
- The total price is 5,000.00 € _____ the _____ charge for air freight.
- Find two shipping documents: insurance _____ and air _____ .
- The sender advises his _____ bank to hand out the documents.
- The goods are packed in _____ boxes.

Crossword

1
2
3
4
5
6
7
8
9
10

Fill in the gaps and complete the crossword.

1. The customer was _____ by the quality of our products.

2. We confirm your order for the items listed _____ .

3. We will _____ the goods as soon as possible.

4. We are pleased to _____ you that we can supply the goods immediately.

5. We can deliver the goods ____ _____ .

6. Your order has been ___ __ ____ and we promise prompt delivery.

7. The goods will be _____ in wooden boxes.

8. We are able to supply the _____ goods within two weeks.

9. We were ____ to read that you were satisfied with our products.

10. We will do our ____ to meet your expectations.

Now write a definition of the hidden word:

_____

_____

123

Draft a letter.

Sie heißen Fred Murray und sind Mitarbeiter der Firma *Telcom*. Sie bearbeiten den Auftrag der Firma *Das Rad*.

- Sie freuen sich, *Das Rad* zu informieren, dass die am .... (siehe *order*) bestellten Waren nun versandbereit sind.

- Die Waren sind jetzt als Container-Teilfracht per Schiff, in seefesten Kisten verpackt, versandt.

- Die Kisten sind an Bord der MS „Mary Anne" verladen worden, die am nächsten Montag planmäßig aus Hull ausläuft.

- *Das Rad* wird die Waren aus dem Container Terminal in Bremen am ... (Datum) abholen können.

- In der Anlage übersenden Sie Ihre Rechnung Nr. 341.

- Da *Das Rad* den Wechsel bereits akzeptiert hat, haben Sie Ihre Korrespondenzbank, *Ibero Platina Bank AG* in Bremen, angewiesen, die Dokumente (Seefrachtbrief, Ursprungszeugnis, Versicherungszertifikat) an *Das Rad* freizugeben.

- Sie hoffen, dass der Auftrag von *Das Rad* zu deren Zufriedenheit ausgeführt worden ist und dass Sie weitere Aufträge von *Das Rad* erhalten werden.

- Grußformel

Here is some help for you.

informieren	to advise
versenden, verschicken	to forward
Container-Teilfracht	part container load
seefest	seaworthy
Kiste	box
verladen	to load
... läuft planmäßig aus ...	... is due to leave ...
Waren abholen	to collect goods
einen Wechsel akzeptieren	to accept a draft
Seefrachtbrief	bill of lading
Ursprungszeugnis	certificate of origin
hoffen, vertrauen	to trust
einen Auftrag ausführen	to carry out an order

Telcom

28 Wakefield Street
Sheffield 8VE17
Tel: 2662042
Fax: 2772042
E-mail:
Telcom@britcom.co.uk

Your ref:
Our ref:
Date:

Choose the right definition and match it with the correct translation.

1	value	a	another word for *price*	1	bestätigen
		b	how much something is worth		
		c	short form of *will you*		
2	acknowledgement	a	a notice to the sender of an order etc. informing him that it has arrived	2	Nettobetrag
		b	*know-how*		
		c	a special prize given to s.b. for his knowledge of s.th.		
3	receipt	a	sit down again	3	Versandabteilung
		b	piece of paper stating s.th. has been paid for		
		c	back seat of a car		
4	net value	a	price you have to pay for a hair net	4	Bestätigung
		b	how nice you think another person is		
		c	how much s.th. is worth without tax		
5	confirm	a	some kind of fir tree	5	versichern, zusichern
		b	to say that sth will definitely happen or has actually happened		
		c	service in a Catholic church		
6	Dispatch Department	a	department responsible for sending the goods to the customers	6	Quittung, Erhalt
		b	department responsible for the litter of a company		
		c	area on a company's premises where broken goods are mended		
7	instruct	a	s.th. you cannot remove from another thing	7	Spediteur
		b	opposite of *extract*		
		c	to tell s.b. what to do		
8	asssure	a	an ancient Middle Eastern people	8	Bezahlung
		b	to be sure you know the right answer		
		c	to cause oneself or others to feel certain about s.th.		
9	attention	a	small fir tree	9	anweisen
		b	special care or action		
		c	a situation in which people feel aggressive towards each other		
10	freight forwarder	a	s.b. who is frightened of s.th.	10	Wert
		b	s.b. who looks forward to s.th.		
		c	s.b. who delivers goods		
11	settlement	a	a place where horse riders keep their saddles	11	Aufmerksamkeit
		b	the action of paying (back) money that is owed		
		c	the time you need to forget s.th.		

Now write down the words from the previous exercise with their definitions and translations.

	Word	Definition	Translation
1			
2			
3			
4			
5			
6			
7			
8			
9			
10			
11			

Fill in the table with suitable verbs and nouns.

Nouns	Verbs	Nouns	Verbs
advice			to deliver
dispatch			to arrive
packing			to supply
agreement			to impress
forwarder			to contain

Now make up sentences and use the words from above.

1. ___
2. ___
3. ___
4. ___
5. ___
6. ___
7. ___
8. ___
9. ___
10. ___
11. ___
12. ___

A Telephone Call

Switchboard: Office Equipment Ltd, good morning. What can I do for you?

Debbie Morris: Good morning. I'd like to speak to Mr Gibson from the purchasing department, please.

Switchboard: Hold the line, please. I'll put you through.

Paul Gibson: Paul Gibson speaking. How can I help you?

Debbie Morris: Good morning, Mr Gibson, this is Debbie Morris from Telecommunications Ltd.

Paul Gibson: Good morning, Ms Morris. Have you already received confirmation of my last order?

Debbie Morris: Yes, thank you. And I can inform you now that the goods are ready for dispatch.

Paul Gibson: Oh, that's good.

Debbie Morris: Yes, but I'm afraid there's a problem concerning the delivery date. You asked for delivery within one week. That won't be possible with our usual means of transport.

Paul Gibson: Hmm ... I see! But we need the goods urgently, because we promised our customer to supply the answering machines at the end of next week.

Debbie Morris: Well, what we could do, is forward the consignment by air freight. But there'll be extra expenses for that.

Paul Gibson: If there is no other way ... but I'll have to discuss that with our manager.

Debbie Morris: Mr Gibson, as we've done business before, I can suggest that the additional costs will be shared between our two companies.

Paul Gibson: That will be fine. In that case I'll accept your proposal. Thank you.

Debbie Morris: You're welcome. I'll call you back when I have details of the exact time when the goods will arrive at your airport.

Paul Gibson: All right, good bye for now.

Debbie Morris: Good bye.

Answer the following questions about the telephone call.

1. What are the two reasons for Debbie Morris' call?
   _____
   _____

2. Why does *Office Equipment* need the goods so urgently?
   _____

3. What is Debbie Morris' proposal to solve the problem?
   _____

4. Why can't Mr Gibson accept the first proposal immediately?
   _____

5. On what basis can Ms Morris offer to share the additional costs equally?
   _____

6. When will Ms Morris call Mr Gibson back?
   _____

Was sagen/schreiben Sie, wenn

a) Sie fragen wollen, ob der Gesprächspartner die Bestätigung Ihrer letzten Bestellung erhalten hat?   _____

b) Sie jdn. informieren wollen, dass die Waren versandbereit sind?   _____

c) Sie bedauern, dass es ein Problem mit dem Liefertermin gibt?   _____

d) Sie einen Vorschlag des Gesprächspartners annehmen?   _____

Crossword

Across

1A	Rechnung
1I	pünktlich (Adv.)
1T	nein
3A	sicher
3H	sein, seine
3S	an, in, zu
4D	Rest
4K	Zustimmung
6A	und
6O	Tag (Mz.)
7F	zur Kenntnis nehmen
7R	das (da), dass
9E	Metall
9O	Waren
10S	auch
11A	du
11F	der, die, das
11J	kräftig, robust
12Q	Anlagen (Kurzw.)
13A	bestätigen
14C	ihr, ihre
16E	seefest
16P	anweisen, raten
18D	Versand
18M	gebraucht, benutzt
19K	Luft
20A	eins
21C	(Auftrags-)bestätigung
21S	Ei

Down

1A	Versicherung
1D	über
1F	Ladung
1I	Preis
1M	zu
1O	dementsprechend (Adv.)
1T	nicht
4K	versichern
4M	packen, verpacken
4R	aufgeführt, gelistet
5U	Hut (Mz)
7H	Händler
8C	rückgabepflichtig
9M	ankommen
9Q	Bestellung
9S	Lager
10U	auf
11J	einige
13A	Bedingung
13F	freigeben
13U	Verkauf
15R	jeder, jede, jedes
16H	was
16M	dein, deine
16T	stark, kräftig
18K	Hand
18P	runter, unten
19C	Meer

Useful phrases: Order Acknowledgements

Opening

Thank you for	your order of ... (see order)	for	.... (products)	to a total
	your order dated ... (see order)		the items listed below	

net value of € .... ,	after the agreed discount of .... %

We were	pleased	to read	that you were	satisfied with	the quality of our products
	glad	to hear		impressed by	

Confirmation

We are glad	to confirm	delivery of the goods	within ... days	of this
This letter is		that our prices and discounts are as follows:		

acknowledgement of your order

Delivery

As	we	can deliver from stock	we	can assure you	that delivery
	the items	are	on stock	are able	to arrange immediate delivery.

will be effected	within ... weeks

You can	expect	the goods	by ..... (date)	at the latest

Our	dispatch department	has been instructed	accordingly
	freight forwarder		

As soon as we	have received	confirmation of your L/C	from our bank	we will

dispatch	the goods

Packing

The goods	will be	packed	in	returnable	containers	
	have been			wooden	cases	with metal bands
				sturdy	boxes	
				seaworthy		

Payment

| We | note | that | settlement | will be | effected | by | irrevocable and confirmed L/C |

| As stated in | our | offer | our terms of payment | are | documents against payment |

Closing

| We | feel | sure | that | the goods | | will meet | your expectations. |
| You | can be | | | he quality of our goods | | | with your approval. |

| We | look forward | to hearing | of | the safe arrival | of your order | and | to receiving |

| further orders | from you | soon |

Useful phrases: Dispatch Notes

Opening

| We | are pleased | to inform | you | that | the goods ordered | are now ready for dispatch |
| | | to advise | | | | |

Dispatch

| The goods | will be sent | by | air freight | as | fast freight |
| | have been forwarded | | ship | | a part container load |

| on | Lufthansa Flight No … | which | leaves | …. (airport) | at … (date). |
| | board MS … | | is due to leave | …. (port) | next week. |

| You | will be able | to collect | the goods | from | the airport | in | (place) | on … (date) |
| | | | | | the port | | | |

Payment / Shipping Documents

| We | have instructed | our correspondent bank | to release | the shipping documents |

| against | payment of the invoice |
| | acceptance of the draft |

Closing

| We | trust | the consignment | will arrive | punctually and in good condition |
| | hope that | your order | has been carried out | to your satisfaction |

133

UNIT SIX: COMPLAINTS

There are many reasons why you might need to write a **letter of complaint;** perhaps you received the wrong goods, or perhaps the goods were damaged. Other reasons might be the wrong quantity, or parts that don't function properly.

When you write your letter of complaint, you should tell the seller **exactly what is wrong** with the goods, e.g.: *Instead of the dynamos we ordered we were sent tyres.* This is important, because the seller needs this information to make a decision and find a solution.

You should include details of your original order, such as: order number, references, date etc., so that the seller knows exactly which consignment you are complaining about.

You can make suggestions to resolve the situation, or you can ask the seller for his/her suggestions, e.g.: *We would appreciate replacements as soon as possible.* Or, *Would you please inform us about what you want us to do with the damaged goods?*

When the seller receives a complaint, they should look into the matter at once. If this takes time a note should be sent to the buyer. Once the situation has been examined the seller can: agree to the buyer's suggestion, refuse the buyer's claim or suggest a compromise. The compromise should be such that both parties can easily agree and resolve the situation as soon as possible.

Mark the following points as *true* or *false*.

	true	false
1. There are many reasons for writing a letter of complaint.	☐	☐
2. You would only write a letter of complaint if the goods arrive late.	☐	☐
3. The seller needs to know what went wrong with the buyer's order.	☐	☐
4. The seller will try to refuse the buyer's claim as soon as possible.	☐	☐
5. Your letter should include all relevant details from your original order.	☐	☐
6. Only the seller can make suggestions to resolve the situation.	☐	☐
7. Always blame the supplier for any mistakes in your order.	☐	☐
8. If the seller receives a complaint, they should wait at least a week.	☐	☐

The Bike Shop

27 Brompton Road
London SW 11
Phone 01-370 2197
Fax   01-370 2198

Das Rad GmbH
Mr Patrick von Zahn
Breite Straße 12
28325 BREMEN
GERMANY

Your ref: PvZ/dl
Our ref: JC/dm
Date: 20 . .

Dear Mr von Zahn

Order No 254

We are writing about the above order which arrived here yesterday.

We regret to tell you that the consignment has given cause for complaints. Due to poor packing 3 bicycles were badly damaged and are unsaleable.

We would appreciate replacements by return of post.

Please let us know what you want us to do with the damaged bicycles.

We look forward to an early reply.

Yours sincerely

John Clease
John Clease
Purchasing Manager

Questions

a) Who is the letter from?
b) Who is the letter to?
c) Why is the sender writing?
d) What is the sender complaining about?
e) What does the sender want to know?
f) What does the sender want *Das Rad* to do?

135

Was sagen/schreiben Sie, wenn

a) Sie **umgehend** um Ersatz bitten?

b) Sie bedauern, dass die Lieferung Anlass zur Beschwerde gegeben hat?

c) Sie mitteilen wollen, dass aufgrund mangelhafter Verpackung die Lieferung beschädigt ist?

d) Sie erklären, dass die beschädigte Ware unverkäuflich ist?

e) Sie um Ersatz bitten?

f) Sie wegen Ihrer Bestellung vom .... schreiben?

g) Ihr Geschäftspartner Ihnen mitteilen soll, was Sie mit der beschädigten Ware tun sollen?

h) Sie sich auf baldige Antwort freuen?

i) Sie mitteilen, dass die Lieferung in der vergangenen Woche eingetroffen ist?

Crossword

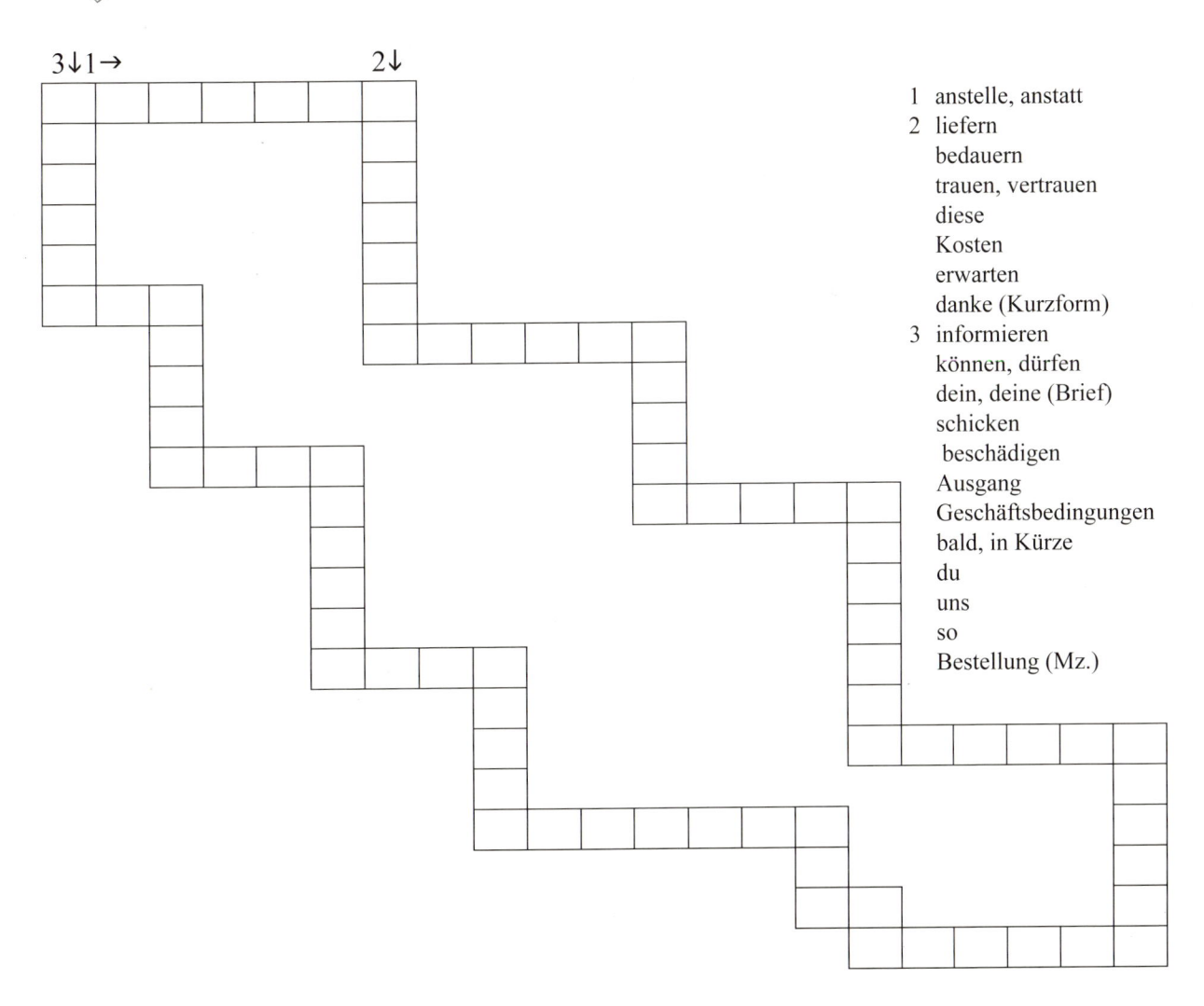

3↓ 1→   2↓

1. anstelle, anstatt
2. liefern
   bedauern
   trauen, vertrauen
   diese
   Kosten
   erwarten
   danke (Kurzform)
3. informieren
   können, dürfen
   dein, deine (Brief)
   schicken
   beschädigen
   Ausgang
   Geschäftsbedingungen
   bald, in Kürze
   du
   uns
   so
   Bestellung (Mz.)

Fill in the gaps by using suitable words from the above crossword.

1. We _____ to _____ you that our order has not arrived yet.
2. We were _____ 500 blue T-shirts _____ of 500 red shorts.
3. We hope to hear from you _____.
4. We _____ replacement by return post.
5. The goods will be sent back to _____ at your _____.
6. Some of the goods were badly _____ _____ that they are unsaleable.
7. We _____ that you will deliver by return post.
8. May we ask you to _____ as soon as possible.

137

Draft a letter.

Sie heißen Inge Langer von der Firma *Das Rad* und schreiben eine Beschwerde an *Lung Mingh Ltd.*, da die Lieferung nicht der Bestellung entspricht.

- Betreff: Bestellung Nr. 367 über 1.000 Dynamos FX 37
- Sie beziehen sich auf die oben angegebene Bestellung, die heute morgen hier angekommen ist.
- Sie bedauern mitteilen zu müssen, dass die falsche Ware geliefert wurde.
- Anstelle der FX 37 Dynamos, die Sie bestellt haben, wurden Ihnen BY 37 Dynamos geschickt.
- Sie sind sicher, dass *Lung Mingh* Ihnen die richtigen Dynamos postwendend zu *Lung Minghs* Lasten zuschickt.
- Bitten Sie darum, die falsche Lieferung abholen zu lassen.
- Sie freuen sich darauf, die Dynamos in Kürze zu erhalten.
- Grußformel

Match the sentences and then write out the letter correctly.

	Yours sincerely		at your expense.
	Instead of the FX 37 dynamos we ordered,		the wrong goods have been delivered.
	We trust that you will send us		Please arrange for the wrong consignment
	to be collected.		we were sent BY 37 dynamos.
	We regret to inform you that		which arrived here this morning.
	the correct dynamos by return post		receiving the dynamos shortly.
	We refer to the above order		Order No 367
	We look forward to		for 1,000 dynamos model FX 37
	Dear Ms Zhang		Das Rad

Das Rad GmbH
Breite Straße 12
28325 Bremen
Tel: +49 421 361-18263
Fax: +49 421 361-18264

Ihr Zeichen: Unser Zeichen: Bremen,

Draft a letter.

Sie heißen Sharon Dearns und arbeiten bei der Firma *Sportmexx*. Leider ist Ihre Bestellung noch nicht eingetroffen. Schreiben Sie eine Beschwerde an die Firma *Sport + Spaß*.

- Betreff: Bestellung Nr. 756

- Beziehen Sie sich auf die oben angegebene Bestellung, die jetzt eine Woche überfällig ist.

- In Ihrer Bestellung hatten Sie darauf hingewiesen, dass die Lieferung innerhalb von 2 Wochen nach Auftragseingang notwendig war.

- Da Sie die Waren dringend benötigen, müssen Sie auf Lieferung bis zum ... *(Datum)* bestehen.

- Sollte *Sport+Spaß* nicht in der Lage sein pünktlich zu liefern, müssen Sie die Waren bei einem anderen Lieferanten bestellen.

- In diesem Fall müssen Sie *Sport + Spaß* für mögliche Extrakosten haftbar machen.

- Grußformel

Here is some help for you.

notwendig	jdn. haftbar machen	darauf hinweisen	in der Lage sein
essential	*to hold someone liable*	*to point out*	*to be able*

in diesem Fall	bestehen auf	eine Woche überfällig
in this case	*to insist on*	*one week overdue*

Sportmexx
43 Station Road
Fakenham
Norfolk NR 12 7 GH
Tel: 876620   Fax: 886620

Your ref:
Our ref:
Date:

Translate the following sentences and fill in the crossword.

1. Wir machen Sie für die Extra-**Kosten** haftbar.
   _____

2. Unsere Bestellung ist **überfällig.**
   _____

3. Sind Sie in der Lage, **pünktlich** zu liefern?
   _____

4. Wir möchten **betonen,** dass wir pünktliche Lieferung erwarten.
   _____

5. Wir werden die Waren bei einem anderen **Lieferanten** bestellen müssen.
   _____

6. Bitte veranlassen Sie die **Auslieferung** so schnell wie möglich.
   _____

7. Wir müssen auf pünktlicher Lieferung **bestehen.**
   _____

8. Lieferung durch Eilzustellung ist **notwendig.**
   _____

9. Wir benötigen die Waren **dringend.**
   _____

142

Fill in the table with suitable verbs and nouns.

Nouns	Verbs	Nouns	Verbs
order			to collect
insistence			to cause
regret			to arrive
information			to return
delivery			to replace
damage			to complain

Now make up sentences and use the words from above.

Example:

1. We would like to **order** the following items:

2. _____
3. _____
4. _____
5. _____
6. _____
7. _____
8. _____
9. _____
10. _____
11. _____
12. _____

There are six hidden words in this wordsquare.

b	r	t	u	n	r	e	f	g	r	e	t	n	u	r	m	o	n	t	g	e	r
i	i	n	s	t	e	a	d	u	t	m	i	s	s	i	n	g	u	t	r	i	n
r	n	e	v	e	g	e	a	r	r	e	t	u	r	i	n	g	o	n	a	l	d
t	r	e	n	t	r	e	r	d	e	t	u	w	q	u	a	n	t	i	t	y	u
k	r	k	l	a	e	w	e	n	t	e	r	r	a	b	l	e	n	t	e	a	r
u	n	f	o	r	t	u	n	a	t	e	l	y	e	n	g	l	a	n	f	n	g
l	b	d	r	i	n	h	g	r	w	d	b	u	z	t	e	r	i	n	u	o	f
c	o	m	q	u	e	s	t	i	b	u	i	n	k	l	o	t	e	w	l	v	b

| 1. anstelle | 2. bedauern | 3. unglücklicherweise |
| 4. fehlende/fehlender | 5. dankbar | 6. Menge |

Draft a letter.

Sie sind die Mitarbeiterin Eva Müller von der Firma *Vobas Computers*. Die von Ihrer Firma bei der Firma *CompaTec* bestellten Waren sind in falschen Mengen geliefert worden. Schreiben Sie eine Beschwerde.

- Betreff: Bestellung Nr. 121

- Sie schreiben wegen der oben angegebenen Bestellung.

- Unglücklicherweise hat *CompaTec* nicht die Mengen geliefert, die Sie bestellt haben.

- Anstelle von 1.000 Soundkarten hat *CompaTec* 1.500 geschickt, und anstelle der 1.500 Paar Lautsprecher schickte *CompaTec* nur 1.000.

- Sie wären dankbar, wenn *CompaTec* die fehlenden Lautsprecher so schnell wie möglich liefern könnte.

- Sie sind bereit, die überzähligen Posten nur gegen einen beträchtlichen Preisnachlass zu behalten.

- Falls dies nicht möglich ist, soll *CompaTec* bitte veranlassen, dass diese Posten abgeholt werden.

- Sie hoffen bald von *CompaTec* zu hören.

- Grußformel

VOBAS COMPUTERS

Pappelstraße 54
28199 Bremen
Tel: +49 421 259292

Ihre Zeichen	Unsere Zeichen	Bremen,

Crossword

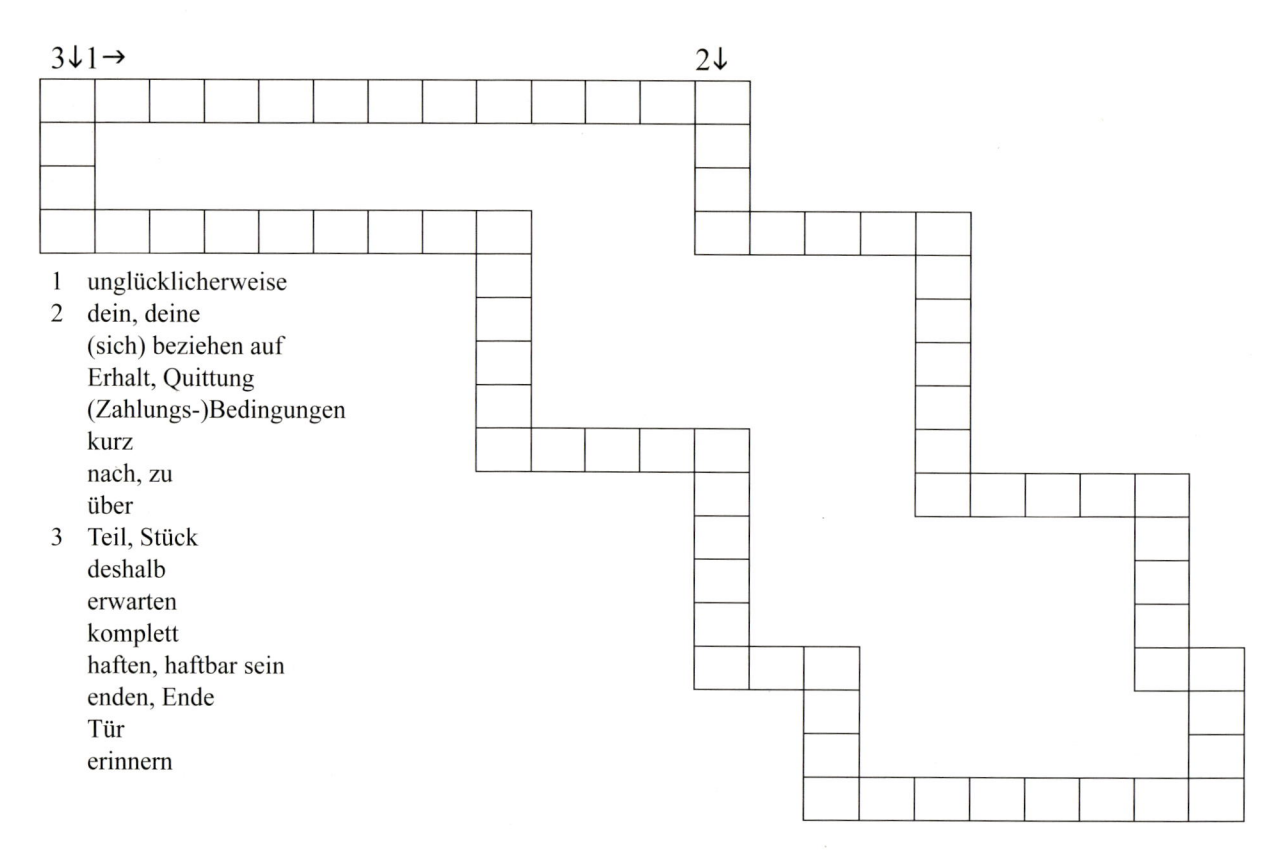

3↓ 1→   2↓

1 unglücklicherweise
2 dein, deine
  (sich) beziehen auf
  Erhalt, Quittung
  (Zahlungs-)Bedingungen
  kurz
  nach, zu
  über
3 Teil, Stück
  deshalb
  erwarten
  komplett
  haften, haftbar sein
  enden, Ende
  Tür
  erinnern

Draft a letter.

Sie sind die Mitarbeiterin Inge Langer von der Firma *Das Rad* und schreiben eine Beschwerde an die Firma *Telcom,* da Sie einige Artikel beschädigt erhalten haben.

- Betreffzeile: Bestellung Nr. 384 über Telefonanlagen

- Sie erhielten die oben angegebene Bestellung heute morgen.

- Unglücklicherweise mussten Sie feststellen, dass aufgrund mangelhafter Verpackung 5 Einheiten des 300 AKH und 7 Einheiten des 217 QHP schwer beschädigt waren.

- Sie wären daher dankbar für Ersatz so schnell wie möglich.

- *Telcom* möge Sie bitte postwendend wissen lassen, wann Sie die Waren erwarten können, da Sie mit der Firma *Technik und Hilfe* Vereinbarungen treffen müssen.

- *Telcom* möge Sie auch bitte darüber informieren, was Sie mit den beschädigten Artikeln tun sollen.

- Sie freuen sich, bald von *Telcom* zu hören.

- Grußformel

Das Rad GmbH
Breite Straße 12
28325 Bremen
Tel : +49 421 361-18263
Fax: +49 421 361-18264

Your ref:
Our ref:
Date: 20 ..

Was sagen/schreiben Sie, wenn

a) Sie wissen wollen, was Sie mit der beschädigten Ware tun sollen?

Would you please let us know what you
- [ ] want to do with the damaged goods?
- [ ] will do with the damaged goods?
- [ ] want us to do with the damaged goods?

b) Sie unglücklicherweise feststellen mussten, dass 3 Teile schwer beschädigt waren?

Unfortunately, we found that 3 items were
- [ ] damaged.
- [ ] bad damaged.
- [ ] badly damaged.

c) Sie so schnell wie möglich Ersatz möchten?

We would appreciate
- [ ] requirements as soon as possible.
- [ ] replacements as soon as possible.
- [ ] requests as soon as possible.

d) Sie postwendend wissen wollen, wann die Ware eintrifft?

Please let us know by
- [ ] post when the goods will arrive here.
- [ ] turn post when the goods will arrive here.
- [ ] return post when the goods will arrive here.

e) Sie aufgrund schlechter Verpackung beschädigte Ware erhalten haben?

Due to
- [ ] poor packing we received damaged goods.
- [ ] poorly packing we received damaged goods.
- [ ] power pack we received damaged goods.

f) Sie wissen wollen, wann Sie die Ware erwarten können?

When can we
- [ ] express the goods?
- [ ] expect the goods?
- [ ] exact the goods?

A Telephone Call

Switchboard:	Telecommunication Ltd, good morning, can I help you?
Paul Gibson:	Good morning, Paul Gibson here, can I speak to Ms Morris in the Sales Department, please?
Switchboard:	Certainly, hold the line, please, I'll put you through.
Debbie Morris:	Good morning. What can I do for you?
Paul Gibson:	Paul Gibson from *Office Equipment* here. Good morning, Ms Morris. We received our order today, but I'm afraid some of the items have been damaged and are unsaleable.
Debbie Morris:	I'm sorry to hear that, Mr Gibson. Could you give me your order number, please?
Paul Gibson:	Yes, it's B 738.
Debbie Morris:	Just a minute, I'll just key that in. – I see, you ordered 200 answering machines and 200 cassettes.
Paul Gibson:	Yes, that's right, but due to poor packing some of the answering machines and cassettes were damaged in transport.
Debbie Morris:	I see. – Now, Mr Gibson, I'll tell you what we can do. If you send me a detailed list of the damaged items, I'll see to the matter at once and we can send you replacements by return post. Would that be alright?
Paul Gibson:	Yes, fine. I'll send the list to you by fax straight away.
Debbie Morris:	… and I'll let you know what to do with the damaged items. We'll have to discuss that with our insurance company first.
Paul Gibson:	No problem, thank you, Ms Morris, good bye.
Debbie Morris:	Good bye, Mr Gibson, and thanks for your call.

Questions

a) What kind of telephone call is the above dialogue?
b) Who is the caller?
c) Who gets the call?
d) What is Mr Gibson complaining about?
e) What does Ms Morris want Mr Gibson to do?
f) What will Mr Gibson send straight away?
g) What does Ms Morris promise to do?
h) Who will Ms Morris have to contact before letting Mr Gibson know what to do with the damaged items?

Translate the following sentences.

Kann ich bitte mit Herrn von Zahn sprechen?

Es tut mir leid, das zu hören.

Einen Moment bitte.

Ich schicke Ihnen die Liste sofort.

Ich sage Ihnen, was wir tun können.

Leider sind einige Artikel beschädigt.

Ich lasse Sie wissen, was Sie mit den Artikeln tun sollen.

Was kann ich für Sie tun?

Wir haben unsere Bestellung heute erhalten.

Ich gebe das eben (in den Computer) ein.

Ich kümmere mich um die Angelegenheit.

Können Sie mir bitte Ihre Bestellnummer geben?

Ich lasse Sie wissen, was Sie mit der beschädigten Ware tun sollen.

Wir müssen das erst mit unserer Versicherung besprechen.

Ich werde sehen, was ich tun kann.

Selbstverständlich.

Aufgrund schlechter Verpackung sind einige Anrufbeantworter beschädigt.

Einige Artikel sind unverkäuflich.

Was sagen/schreiben Sie, wenn

a) Sie fragen, ob Sie mit Frau Müller von der Verkaufsabteilung sprechen können?

   Can I
   - [ ] speak Frau Müller in the Sales Department, please?
   - [ ] speak to Frau Müller in the Sales Department, please?
   - [ ] to speak Frau Müller in the Sales Department, please?

b) Sie bedauern mitteilen zu müssen, dass einige Artikel beschädigt sind?

   I'm afraid
   - [ ] of the damaged items.
   - [ ] of some of the damaged items.
   - [ ] some of the items are damaged.

c) Sie etwas in den Computer eingeben wollen?

   I'll just
   - [ ] put my key in.
   - [ ] key that in.
   - [ ] look for my key.

d) Sie mitteilen, dass sie sich um die Angelegenheit kümmern werden?

   I'll
   - [ ] see that nothing matters.
   - [ ] see the matter.
   - [ ] see to the matter.

e) Sie Ihren Gesprächspartner wissen lassen werden, was er mit der beschädigten Ware tun soll?

   I'll let you
   - [ ] know the damaged items.
   - [ ] know about the damaged items.
   - [ ] know what to do with the damaged items.

f) Sie mitteilen, dass einige Artikel unverkäuflich sind?

   Some items are
   - [ ] not for sale.
   - [ ] not on sale.
   - [ ] unsaleable.

Crossword

Across

- 1A Verpackung
- 1J unglücklicherweise
- 2E nein
- 3O existieren
- 4H wirklich, real
- 5B er
- 5P beschädigen, Beschädigung
- 6C beträchtlich
- 7N Paar
- 9A Grund, Anlass
- 9Q Fall
- 10E Handlung, Aktion
- 11N Kosten, Lasten, Ausgaben
- 12A fest
- 12G informieren
- 13Q Name (Mz.)
- 14G für
- 15A mittel
- 15L Aufmerksamkeit
- 16G sein, seine
- 18A überzählig
- 18J postwendend

Down

- 1A arm, schlecht
- 1C abholen, (ein)sammeln
- 1E in
- 1L oder
- 1S Zusatzkosten
- 4H (Preis-)nachlass, Ermäßigung
- 4K haften, haftbar sein
- 5E anstelle, anstatt
- 5N Ersatz
- 5Q Luft
- 5U Ausgang
- 9A bestätigen
- 10L Beschwerde
- 12J Formular (Mz.)
- 13Q Zur Kenntnis nehmen
- 15C Liebe, Lieber (im Brief)
- 16G (er/sie) hat

Useful phrases: Complaints

Opening

We	are writing about	the above-mentioned order	which	arrived here	yesterday this morning
	refer to			is now	one week four days	overdue

Why are we writing?

We	regret to inform you	that	the consignment	has given cause for complaint
			the wrong goods	have been delivered

Unfortunately	you did not	supply	the quantities	we ordered			
	we found	that	due to	poor packing	3 bicycles	were	badly	damaged

What do we want?

As we	need	the goods	urgently	we must		insist on		dispatch by …
We would		therefore	appreciate	replacements	by return post as soon as possible			
		be grateful	if you	could supply	the missing	items	as soon as possible	

What else do we want?

Please	let us know	by return post	when we can expect the goods			
Would you also please	inform us	what you want	us to do	with the	damaged	goods items

Please arrange for	the	wrong	consignmet	to be collected

We	trust	that you	will send us	the correct	dynamos	by return post	at your expense

Further information

We	are willing	to keep	the	surplus	items	at a	considerable	reduction in price

If	you	are	not able	to deliver	on time	we	will	have to	order	from another	supplier

Vocabulary Unit by Unit

Unit 1 LAYOUT OF A LETTER

actual	eigentlich, tatsächlich
additional	zusätzlich
addressee	Adressat, Empfänger
attention line	Zeile mit Angabe des Empfängers
best wishes	Viele Grüße
body of the letter	Brieftext
company	Firma
complimentary close	(höfliche) Grußformel
date	Datum
Dear	Lieber, Liebe (Anrede im Brief)
Dear Sir or Madam	Sehr geehrte Damen und Herren
enclosure/enc	Anlage
inside address	Adresse
layout	Gestaltung, Aufmachung
letterhead	Briefkopf
opening salutation	(höfliche) Anrede
particular	besonders, bestimmt
a particular person	eine bestimmte Person
reference	Referenz(zeichen)
responsible	verantwortlich
signature (block)	Unterschrift
subject line	Betreff, Überschrift
to vary	unterscheiden, abweichen
Yours faithfully	Mit freundlichen Grüßen
Yours sincerely	Mit freundlichen Grüßen

Unit 2 ENQUIRIES

a leading company	ein führendes Unternehmen
to avoid	vermeiden
a well-established firm	ein gut eingeführtes Unternehmen
additional	zusätzlich
advertisement	Anzeige, Werbung
advisable	ratsam
available	verfügbar
to be legally binding	verbindlich sein
to belong to s.th.	zu etwas zugehörig sein
business relations	Geschäftsbeziehungen
to call back	zurückrufen (tel.)
catalogue	Katalog
comprehensive	umfassend
conditions	Bedingungen
current	aktuell
customer	Kunde
decision	Entscheidung
delivery	Lieferung
department	Abteilung
to describe	beschreiben

to develop	entwickeln, erschließen
to draft	entwerfen
in due course	demnächst
to equip	ausstatten
edition	(Zeitungs-)Ausgabe
enquiry	Anfrage
expectation	Erwartung
factory; plant	Fabrik
fair	Messe
for testing	zu Testzwecken
further information	weitere Informationen
general	allgemein
to be grateful	dankbar sein
Head Office	Hauptverwaltung, Zentrale
to install	einbauen, installieren
intercom (system)	Gegensprechanlage
to be interested in s.th.	sich für etwas interessieren
to let s.b have s.th.	jdm. etwas zur Verfügung stellen
line of business	Branche
manufacturer	Hersteller
medium-sized	mittelständisch
our representative	unser Vertreter
particularly; especially	besonders
permanent	ständig
to be pleased	erfreut sein
please let us know ...	bitte lassen Sie uns wissen
price list	Preisliste
quantity discount	Mengenrabatt
range of products	Sortiment von Produkten
recent, recently	neu, vor kurzem, neulich, kürzlich
recommend	empfehlen
to be reliable	zuverlässig sein
requirement	Anforderung, Bedürfnis, Bedarf
to meet the requirements	den Anforderungen entsprechen
retailer	Einzelhändler
sample	Muster
service	Dienstleistung
source of supply	Bezugsquelle
special delivery	Eilzustellung
to summarise	zusammenfassen
supplier	Lieferant
to supply (v) / supply (n)	liefern / Lieferung, Versorgung
terms of payment	Zahlungsbedingungen
to pay in cash	bar bezahlen
to quote a price	Preis nennen
to receive	erhalten
to refer to s.th.	sich auf etwas beziehen
to require	benötigen
to send	verschicken

steady	ständig
to stay the same	gleich bleiben, sich nicht ändern
to trade	handeln
together	zusammen
we look forward to hearing from you soon	wir freuen uns, bald von Ihnen zu hören
wholesaler	Großhändler

Unit 3 OFFERS

air freight	Luftfracht
approval	Zustimmung
to draw s.b.'s attention to sth	jds. Aufmerksamkeit auf etwas lenken
to do business	Geschäfte machen
casual clothes	Freizeitkleidung
charge	Gebühr
cash discount	Barzahlungsrabatt, Skonto
computer component	Computerbauteil
to confirm (v) / confirmation (n)	bestätigen (einer Information) / Bestätigung
to contact	kontaktieren, in Verbindung setzen
to decide	entscheiden, sich entschließen
documents against payment	Dokumente gegen Bezahlung
to expand	expandieren, ausweiten
to meet s.b.'s expectations	jds. Erwartungen entsprechen
ex works	ab Werk
to feature	(heraus)bringen
firm	fest
first order discount	Erstauftragsrabatt
further	weitere, weiterer (Rabatte, Rabatt etc.)
to hesitate	zögern
high-quality	qualitativ hochwertig
to identify	identifizieren
in favour of	zu Gunsten von
to include	beinhalten
to indicate	bezeichnen, zeigen, andeuten
installation	Einbau
irrevocable	unwiderruflich
leaflet	Werbezettel
letter of credit	(Dokumenten-)Akkreditiv
to meet with s.b.'s approval	jds. Zustimmung finden
net price	Nettopreis
non-binding	nicht bindend, unverbindlich
offer	Angebot
order	Bestellung
order form	Bestellformular
packing	Verpackung
payment	Bezahlung, Begleichung
payment should be made by ...	die Zahlung soll per ... erfolgen
to effect payment	Zahlung leisten
payment should be effected by ...	die Zahlung soll per ... geleistet werden
quotation	(Preis-)Angebot

raw materials	Rohmaterialien
receipt	Erhalt (auch: Quittung, Einnahmen)
retail discount	Einzelhandelsrabatt
shipment	Versand, Verschiffung
special offer	Sonderangebot
telephone system	Telefonanlage
to place an order	eine Bestellung aufgeben
to point out	betonen, auf etwas hinweisen
to be prepared to do s.th.	bereit sein etwas zu tun
to present	präsentieren, zeigen, vorführen
to quote (a price)	einen Preis nennen, angeben
to regret	bedauern
to request	wünschen
seaworthy	seefest
to be subject to	einer Sache unterworfen sein
to submit	vorlegen, einreichen, hier: übermitteln
trade discount	Händlerrabatt
under separate cover	mit getrennter Post
up-market	anspruchsvoll
video phone	Bildtelefon
to be willing to do s.th.	bereit sein, etwas zu tun
to be worth	wert sein

Unit 4 ORDERS

after receipt of the goods	nach Erhalt der Ware
agreed terms	vereinbarte Bedingungen
agreement	Vereinbarung
to arrange delivery	Lieferung veranlassen
to make arrangements for s.th. to be done	veranlassen, dass etwas getan wird
to assure	jdm. etwas versichern, zusichern
at the latest	spätestens
binding order	verbindliche Bestellung
business relations	Geschäftsbeziehungen
to cancel s.th.	rückgängig machen, widerrufen
to confirm in writing	schriftlich bestätigen
to deliver from stock	ab Lage liefern
to demand (v) / demand (n)	fordern / Nachfrage
to draft (v) / draft (n)	entwerfen / Entwurf
to effect payment	bezahlen
to expect (v) / expectation (n)	erwarten / Erwartung
to grant a discount	Rabatt gewähren
to be impressed	beeindruckt sein
initial order	Erstbestellung
to make some notes	ein paar Notizen machen
to note (v) / note (n)	zur Kenntnis nehmen / Notiz
Payment has to be made by ...	Die Zahlung soll/muss per ... erfolgen
please find enclosed ...	in der Anlage finden Sie .../übersenden wir ...
to be prepared to do s.th.	bereit sein, etwas zu tun
previous	ehemalig, vorherig

to receive (v) / receipt (n)	erhalten / Erhalt
repeat order	Nachbestellung
to reply (v) / reply (n)	(be)antworten / Antwort
returnable	rückgabepflichtig
safe arrival	sichere Ankunft
satisfactory	zufriedenstellend
to settle the invoice	die Rechnung begleichen
settlement	Bezahlung (auch: Siedlung)
shortly	in Kürze
to state	deklarieren, angeben
thank you for your trouble	danke für Ihre Bemühungen
trial order	Probebestellung
urgent (adj) / urgently (adv)	dringend
valid	gültig
this order is only valid if ...	diese Bestellung gilt nur, wenn ...
within XYZ days	innerhalb (binnen) XYZ Tagen

Unit 5 ORDER ACKNOWLEDGEMENT

accordingly (adv)	(dem)entsprechend
acknowledgement	Bestätigung
advice of dispatch	Versandanzeige
air freight	Luftfracht
to arrive (v) / arrival (n)	ankommen / Ankunft
to assure	etwas zusichern
bill of lading	Frachtbrief, Konnossement
to carry out	durchführen
certificate of origin	Ursprungszeugnis
to collect	abholen, einsammeln
confirmation	Bestätigung
dispatch note	Versandanzeige
to do one's best	sein Bestes tun
draft (n)	Wechsel, Tratte (auch: Entwurf)
fast freight	Eillieferung
to forward	befördern
in good condition	in gutem Zustand
in stock	vorrätig sein, auf Lager haben
to instruct	anweisen, informieren
to instruct s.b. accordingly	jdn. entsprechend informieren / anweisen
insurance certificate	Versicherungsschein, - zertifikat
item	(Rechnungs-)Posten, Stück, Gegenstand
listed below	unten aufgelistet
to load	laden
to meet with s.b.'s approval	jds. Zustimmung finden
orders worth at least ... €	Bestellungen in Höhe von mindestens ... €
to pack	packen, verpacken
part container load	Container-Teilfracht
purpose	Zweck, Grund
to be ready for dispatch	versandbereit sein
to release the documents	die Dokumente freigeben

returnable	rückgabepflichtig
to be satisfied with s.th.	mit etwas zufrieden sein
settlement	Begleichung
shipping documents	Versanddokumente
stock	Lager (auch: Aktien)
to deliver from stock	vom Lager liefern
safe	sicher
sturdy	kräftig, stämmig
The ship is due to leave on Monday	Das Schiff läuft planmäßig am Montag aus
to trust	davon ausgehen, vertrauen
You can be sure that ...	Sie können sicher sein, dass ...

Unit 6 Complaints

above	oben
above-mentioned	oben angegeben
to appreciate	zu schätzen wissen
as soon as possible	so schnell wie möglich
at once	umgehend
case / in this case	Fall / in diesem Fall
to cause (v) / cause (n)	verursachen / Ursache
to make a claim	einen Schadensersatzanspruch anmelden
to complain (v) / complaint (n)	sich beschweren / Beschwerde
considerable	beträchtlich, erheblich
consignment	Sendung, Ladung
to damage (v) / damage (n)	beschädigen / Beschädigung
due to	aufgrund von, wegen
essential	notwendig, unabdingbar
to examine	untersuchen
expense	Kosten
at your expense	auf Ihre Kosten, zu Ihren Lasten
to inform	informieren
to insist on	bestehen auf
instead (of)	anstelle, anstatt (von)
to key s.th. in	etwas in den Computer eingeben
to hold s.b. liable	jdn. haftbar machen
letter of complaint	Beschwerdebrief
to look into the matter	der Sache (Angelegenheit) nachgehen
overdue	überfällig
at a reduction in price	mit einem Preisnachlass
to refuse	ablehnen
to regret	bedauern
replacement	Ersatz
by return post	postwendend
solution	Lösung
to suggest (v) / suggestion (n)	vorschlagen / Vorschlag
surplus	überzählig
to trust	vertrauen, hier: davon ausgehen
unfortunately	unglücklicherweise
...what you want us to do with ...	...was wir mit ... machen sollen

Notes: